HEARERS OF THE WORD

HEARERS
OF THE WORD

KARL RAHNER

Translated by
Michael Richards

HERDER AND HERDER

1969
HERDER AND HERDER NEW YORK
232 Madison Avenue, New York, N. Y. 10016

Original edition: *Hörer des Wortes,*
Munich, Kösel-Verlag, 1963
This edition revised by J. B. Metz.

Nihil obstat: Leo J. Steady, Censor Librorum
Imprimatur: ✠ Robert F. Joyce, Bishop of Burlington
October 23, 1968

Library of Congress Catalog Card Number: 69-14389
© 1969 by Herder and Herder, Inc.
Manufactured in the United States

CONTENTS

PART FOUR
THE PLACE WHERE THE FREE MESSAGE IS FOUND

PART FIVE
CONCLUSION

PREFACE

The first edition of this work appeared in the war year of 1941. The unpropitious time of its appearance may in no small way have contributed to the fact that the sketch presented here has not heretofore been fully appreciated in the debate on philosophy of religions. A glance at the more recent works on the subject, on both the Catholic and the Protestant side, corroborate the truth of this assertion. With the passing of the years the title of the book became more current than its content. As far as I know there are up to now only two authors who concern themselves rather expressly with the theses put forth therein. They are H. Robbers, who in the preface to his work *Wijsbegeerte en Openbaring* (Utrecht-Brussels, 1948) attests that he was substantially influenced by the book, and this especially in the first three main parts of his work (see pp. 11 ff.); and H. Fries, who in the second part of his thesis *Die katholische Religionsphilosophie der Gegenwart* (Heidelberg, 1949) discusses, among other things, this book by Karl Rahner (see pp. 253-260).

Since the author has been kept by various circumstances from presenting a new edition of the present work, which has been out of print for years, although always in demand, I have, in accordance with his wishes and upon agreement with the publisher, taken on gratefully and gladly the task of preparing this new edition. Before going into particulars about the nature and extent of its content, I would like to indicate briefly the basic thought-content of the work itself, to which this new edition should remain dedicated. *Hearers of the Word*—that biblical determination of man vis-à-vis revelation—is here to be recaptured in a sketch of the philosophy of religion which comes close to the thought of Thomas Aquinas but at the same time takes into account the problems and attempted solutions of modern religious philosophers. Man hereby becomes visible as that being which comes into self-recognition by means of history (just as history itself comes into its own only by way of man); man must listen in on history in order to encounter there the "word" that founds and enlightens existence, this word to which the perceptive reason of man has always been questioningly attuned. The founding of a faith-grounded existence upon the historical word of God, therefore, is not arbitrary in the least; in fact, it co-responds in a deep and fundamental way to this existence.

The present work, which falls into the category of "funda-mental-theological anthropology," is concerned with an idealistic piece of philosophical enlightenment in matters of faith, some-thing that seems the more urgent in our times as the basic relation of man to history loses more and more ground to the categorical pre-eminence of science and technology as an ideal system of epistemology, and as the modern individual first of all looks upon the founding of existence and his own perplexity in the face of it, in a historical context, with skepticism or in-comprehension.

How, then, are we to describe the scope and extent of the new edition? Since the individual chapters of the original com-prised an equivalent number of lectures in which, of necessity, the lecture material often had to be repeated—especially at the beginning of each successive lecture and at the end by way of a summary, the text for the new edition had to be condensed and in no small part abridged. Thus one chapter (the original chapter 14) is left out entirely; what remained of new material was in-corporated into the foregoing chapter (13).

However, due to a fair number of corrections and more or less substantial additions to the text, the compass of the original was not only equalled but surpassed. The most important of these corrections and expansions of content can be considered as fall-ing within two groups, defined respectively by an ontological and a theological point of view. The theological viewpoint is con-cerned with the non-definitive quality and need for completion of the work through a "philosophy of religion contingent on theology." The concept of revelation itself was differentiated by distinguishing between "transcendental" and "categorical" revelation; the essential unity of revelation and grace was emphasized; and finally a more exact determination of the mutual immanence of grace and nature, revelation and reason, theological and philosophical act in the original and ever-whole unity of the historical subjectivity of man was attempted. This aspect of the corrections is rather more apparent in the notes than in the text; to pursue it consistently in the text itself, in all its details and ramifications, would be to repeat the entire outline of the problem from the starting-point of theology. I have indicated this to be an unfinished task at the end of the book.

The ontological viewpoint is concerned with the attempt to follow through yet more closely the problem already broached— the question of existence—and with thereby making the logical allowances for an objectivistic-hypothesizing misunderstanding of "being." To this end we concern ourselves primarily with a fundamentally new conception of the "analogy of being" (as the "analogy of having-being") and the so-called "ontological difference" (based on the difference between a completed and an incompleted "ontological difference"). Besides introducing the concept of "transcendental-liminal experience" we should here include references to the problem of the relation between transcendence and historicity of the human spirit, as well as, finally, attempting to bring the Thomistic concept of the concrete world "up to date" with the more original concept of a personal world. This aspect of the question was incorporated into the text throughout. Of course the original sketch should remain unobscured, and I hope this is so in those instances where I myself tried to add some fairly substantial emendations to the ontological outlines of the statement. The author assured me of his approval as regards the type and scope of the editing; nevertheless, I alone bear the full responsibility for this new revised edition.

To avoid materially exceeding the original compass of the work, a discussion of the literature on the philosophy of religion is not included here. In the notes, frequent references is made (without naming the author) to later writings of Karl Rahner in which the following sketch is expanded or taken up anew from different points of view. Wherever I thought it necessary to the end of establishing facts or developing the edited text, I have allowed myself to refer also to my own publications where applicable.

I hope to have succeeded in the task of revising to the extent that it could express modestly the thanks I will always owe to the author.

Johannes B. Metz

PART ONE

THE ENQUIRY

1. AN ENQUIRY INTO PHILOSOPHY OF RELIGION
as the Ontology
of the "Potentia Oboedientialis" for Revelation

What is meant by the philosophy of religion, and what I hope to achieve by attempting to provide a foundation for such a philosophy of religion, can be most clearly defined by comparing and contrasting the science which we call philosophy of religion with another science—theology, with which it seems to have the closest relationship, from the point of view of affinity as well as hostility.

The study of the relationship between these sciences would seem at first, however, to be a highly academic and completely harmless affair, an occupation in which two sciences give an account of one another's presence, autonomy, dignity, and nobility; for the discussion of the relationship between two sciences seems to presuppose that the two sciences exist, and that we know what each is in itself. Only thus, it would seem, can we talk sensibly about their relationship to one another. Hence the definition of their relationship seems to be a matter of second degree, an extra of no special importance.

In fact, however, the matter is not so simple. Beneath an apparently innocent problem of scientific theory, that of the relationship between the two sciences, lies the prior foundation and essential constitution of the two sciences themselves. This foundation is present in such a way that its very existence must be the concern of the enquirer.

Certainly, at the start of our discussion of the relationship between two sciences we must already know in some sense what we have begun to talk about. We must always possess a provi-

3

sional knowledge of what in each case the science is all about. This is not to say that whoever has such a knowledge of the practice of the science must necessarily have grasped its true nature. In any such exploratory acquaintance with the subject-matter of the science, what this subject-matter *really* is, and what scientific enquiry into definitions of the subject-matter *really* hopes to achieve, can nonetheless, in the last analysis, be hidden and remain hidden, in spite of all the advances of the science. Each separate empirical science brings apriorily to the inauguration of its enquiry an antecedent law in terms of which it seeks to examine the definitions of its subject-matter. In the prosecution of the various sciences today there is a widespread failure to recognize this *a priori* prejudgment of the direction of scientific work, but this does not disprove the presence of such a prejudgment. On the contrary, it is a sign of how such an *a priori* attitude is taken for granted by the particular sciences, and of how little the sciences are aware of the metaphysical foundation upon which they rest. We learn from the mere results of a science how, according to these results, the subject-matter of that science is to be defined *in its details,* but not why and with what justification it conceives the particular way in which it sets about, apriorily, to investigate the subject-matter, so as to be able to determine what it is in general. From practicing a science we can learn how to manipulate it, that is, we can learn its method, but we cannot in the least learn why and with what aim man practices that science in the first place.[1]

Such questions concerning the theory of science precede the particular science in fact if not in time. Hence they are not retrospective thoughts about a science but its very basis, both in respect of subject-matter and of the specific reason for, and in the manner of, its investigation. Insofar, therefore, as the very first beginnings of a science are to be found in a theoretical question about science, the science in question, considered on its own, cannot direct us to the place where this theoretical question may find an answer. A particular science rests ultimately upon a foun-

[1] See "Wissenschaft als 'Konfession'?", in *Schriften zur Thelogie* III, Einsiedeln, 1956, pp. 455-472; see also J. B. Metz, "Weisheit," in *Handbuch theologischer Grundbegriffe* II, München, 1963, pp. 805-813.

dation which it did not itself lay. Such a foundation is what makes it possible for that science to exist at all.

The *principium* of answering a question about the theory of science must be the same *in all cases*. The same multiplicity of heterogeneous principles should not re-appear behind the plurality of the sciences to be established. This would result in failure to achieve the original and continuously experienced unity of the thinking and acting subject. This implies, however, that the foundation of the sciences in the theory of science is *one,* as Aristotle has already observed in Book IV of his *Metaphysics.*[2] There is, then, a unified fundamental science, which first of all gives to the particular sciences their various subject-matters in their several *a priori,* presupposed structures, and the resulting formal principles through which the subject-matter is known. It is this unified science which simultaneously must establish these sciences at their very origin as open to human understanding in its necessity and uniqueness. The old name for this *epistēmē protē* is "metaphysics." We conclude, therefore, that all questions about the theory of science are questions pertaining to the one, first science—metaphysics.

If, then, the sciences in their necessity are originally founded (that is, become determined as to their subject-matter, peculiarity, and necessity) in a unified, although as yet obscure, substratum, it becomes clear that the question of the *relationship* between two sciences is a *metaphysical* question. It is metaphysical, moreover, not in the sense that metaphysics is able ultimately to reflect also upon the relationship between two sciences, but in the sense that metaphysics has in fact originally placed these sciences in a relationship, to the extent that it constituted these particular sciences at the very start. For the plurality of sciences must arise from this unified basis laid by metaphysics. Hence we can say, conversely: the question about the relationship between two sciences is not one about a linking or setting in a relationship which is extraneous to their specific constitutions, but it is the question about their unity within one and the same metaphysical foundation. To the extent, however, that it is

[2] Aristotle, *Metaphysics* IV, 1 and 4.

the very plurality of the sciences which makes the question about their unified foundation most obvious and most difficult, and that it is in terms of the plurality of the sciences that a reason for the question appears most clearly and comprehensively—to this extent the problem of the relationship between two sciences is the most difficult and also most penetrating when it is applied to the theoretical constitution of these sciences, each in its own domain. Ultimately, then, the question about the relationship between two sciences is the question about the theoretical foundation of the individual sciences, each in its own way, but upon the same metaphysical substratum. Summing up what has been said so far, we may conclude: the theoretical question about the relationship between two sciences must in the end be understood as the metaphysical question about the single cause of origin which determines both sciences in the peculiarity of their subject-matter, and in the individual necessity of each, thus placing the two in a definite relationship to one another.

Insofar as a question pertaining to the theory of science is always at the same time a question about the specific nature of science as a *human* activity, it is always also a metaphysical question about the nature of man. For a science is grasped in terms of its foundation only when it ceases to be conceived as a framework of propositions (a system) valid in themselves, and comes to be seen as the characteristic activity of that human being who thinks these propositions, and must think them.[3] But because a theoretical definition of man is always of necessity a prejudgment of how man ought existentially to act, a question pertaining to the theory of science is, therefore, no harmless curiosity about something or other, but an existential concern of man himself.

Whatever be made in general of the meaning of a question

---

[3] Science is a basic process of human existence insofar as, in its reflexivity, it never simply supervenes existence already adequately constituted, but (under one form or another) emerges of necessity in the incipience of the one historical existence. Man always has need of a reflex-thematic relationship of some sort to himself, and thereby to the whole of his world. All the same, this necessary incipience of "science" as reflexion remains in constant variation to its one and ever whole origin, in whose luminosity this reflexion takes place.

pertaining to the theory of science, let us now turn to the problem that presents itself here, the problem of the relationship between theology and the philosophy of religion. This problem is the metaphysical question about the one foundation upon which each science in its own way is constituted for the first time, and so it is also the question about the nature of man as the existent being who must of necessity practice these sciences.

Having thus formulated our theme, we already see the fundamental difficulty into which we have fallen by conceiving it in this fashion. This difficulty has two aspects.

(1) Let us first of all relate the provisional knowledge which we possess of the two sciences to the above formulation of our theme.

(a) The *philosophy of religion* (thus we may designate our knowledge of the first of the two sciences, presupposing, that is, the usual Catholic view of the philosophy of religion [4]) is the knowledge which man *on his own* is able to acquire of the correct relation of man to God as Absolute. For classical Christian philosophy of religion, however, knowledge of God, upon which a philosophy of religion that wishes to be more than merely descriptive history of religion and psychology of religion essentially depends, and in which it has in fact already reached its limit, is no static, self-contained science, but a profound element of ontology in general. It is not possible here, nor is it necessary, to prove this proposition fully. Ultimately, the proof lies in the fact that God is not a datum which can be directly grasped in his true self by man and his experience. For metaphysical perception, God is seen as the absolute cause of existent things and of the knowledge of being. He is revealed every time

[4] While Catholic scholastic philosophy usually understands philosophy of religion as the foundation of "natural religion" derived from "natural theology," the concept of philosophy of religion is elsewhere primarily conceived of as philosophical reflection of the historically, psychologically, and phenomenologically exalted fact of concrete religions. In this connection also, of course, the question of the normative limitations upon the comprehension of such reflexion comes to the fore; thus it testifies to the inevitability, although not to the exclusivity, of the conception of religious philosophy that has its effect on Catholic-scholastic philosophy, a conception which, in turn, obviously stands in danger of obscuring for itself the spiritual horizon of its metaphysical sketch.

man enquires into anything which exists, but who remains knowable only as the remote cause of that which is. In the phrase of St. Thomas, God can be presented only as the *principium* of that which is, and the science of God can never be the *subiectum* of a specific, purely human science.[5] Having made this presupposition we face a question and a difficulty. On the one hand, we are to base the philosophy of religion as science upon metaphysics according to the theory of science; on the other hand, the science with which we are dealing in this case is nothing other than that same metaphysics upon which it is supposed to rest.

And so in this case the foundation in terms of the theory of science of the science here in question, is in the end none other than the self-establishment of metaphysics; and our question about the scientific-theoretical foundation of the philosophy of religion becomes the question about metaphysics itself and its constitution. The question about the philosophy of religion becomes the question as to why man pursues metaphysics and being, and how human metaphysics can reach up to God.

(b) But our question assumes an even more difficult form when we relate our provisional knowledge of *theology* to the above formulation of our theme. In its *original* nature theology is not really some kind of science, the constitution of which is created by man himself. In its origin it is always the self-illuminating hearing of the revelation of God himself, which proceeds from God's free decree, through his own word. In the primary and original sense theology is not a system of valid propositions constituted by human thought, but the totality of divine speech [6] addressed by God himself to man, albeit in human language. This word of God's revelation thus already heard, and grasped

[5] See *In Boeth. de Trin.* 5, 4 and *In Met. Provem.*

[6] "Speech" is here to be taken in the comprehensive sense. It is not meant only or even primarily in the sense of the actual word (of the "prophets"), but above all as referring to that "revelation" which is transmitted to the transcendental openness of man through the gracious self-revealing of God, and while, occurring in time and space in the events of salvation history, necessarily appears as word and deed. See "Weltgeschichte und Heilsgeschichte," in *Schriften zur Theologie* V, Einsiedeln, 1962, pp. 115-135.

in an original unity of *auditus* and *intellectus,* can and should in turn be made by man the object of his enquiring, systematizing thought. It should be fitted into the whole complex of human science, thus creating a second form of theological science. The difference between theology in the first and in the second sense may be described in old-fashioned terminology as the distinction between positive and scholastic theology. But such a science of scholastic theology always rests essentially upon the free revelation and hearing of the word of God himself, that is, upon positive theology.[7]

This simple hearing and accepting of a message from the God who is exalted high above this world, and thus freely discloses himself; this hearing of a message which is of incalculable content, and which cannot be discovered by man for himself, would seem (because resting upon an act of God upon which the hearing essentially depends) to be fundamentally beyond the reach of scientific-theoretical foundation. This revelation of God cannot be given a foundation by man, neither in its actuality or necessity nor in its inner essence. If this is true, it is clear from the start that a scientific-theoretical foundation for theology, which can at least be conceived as in some sense *preparatory* to theology, can *cover* not the word of God, but the hearing of the word of God by man, and this only with regard to the *a priori* possibility of the capacity to hear a revelation which might conceivably proceed from God. It is immediately obvious that a scientific-theoretical foundation of revelational theology, which precedes theology itself, cannot hope to provide more than this. Thus, too, it must still remain doubtful (at least for the moment) *whether* and in what sense man is able to discover within himself some kind of "ear" for a revelation which might possibly proceed from God, *before* he has in fact heard something and come to know thereby that he can hear; and *how* this capacity to hear

---

[7] Here it is presupposed that the hearing of the word of revelation constituted by God's grace in the self-realization of man is an *interior* moment of the manifestation of the word of God itself. See J. B. Metz, "Theologische und metaphysische Ordnung," in *ZkTh* 83 (1961), pp. 1-14.

within his constitution has to be interpreted, in terms of the revelation granted.[8]

Thus if now and in future *we* speak of a scientific-theoretical foundation of theology, in every case we use the term in the sense of a demonstration of the possibility in man of hearing the message, insofar as this is possible in terms of our explicitly restricted starting point.[9] It is evident, therefore, that our question is not about man as a true theologian, but about man as that existent being to whom the possibility of becoming a theologian essentially belongs, *if* the free incalculable message of God is sent out to him and *if,* by grace and its historical appearance in the Word, he is granted (for the first time) the full *capacity* to hear.

Whether the sole requirement for the constitution of a genuine theology in man is that the message confront man in the form

[8] In light of factual Christian revelation, the concrete ability to hear the divine word of revelation is constituted by two moments: by the spiritual transcendence of man (his "subjectivity"), and by its "elevation" through grace, or its "illumination." On the "supernatural existential" see "Ueber das Varhältnis von Natur und Gnade," in *Schriften zur Theologie* I, Einsiedeln, 1954; see also *Schriften zur Theologie* IV (1960), pp. 209-236. Since this "supernaturalexistential" does not imply a new, added ability, but an inner illumination of spiritual subjectivity or transcendence itself without admitting the possibility of being created as such from it, the ability to hear the word of revelation can be considered in the light of the basic constitution of the human spirit. At the same time the methodological restriction to this aspect must not illicitly and prematurely abridge the analysis of this ability to hear, for the incipient reflection under this aspect will not and cannot of its own accord lay claim to being "purely metaphysical" in a theological sense, because on the one hand, metaphysical reflexion is of its nature always enclosed in an uncontrollable historical situation which cannot be adequately retrieved in its reflexivity and is, moreover, present to itself in this very uncontrollability, and because on the other hand, the "supernatural existential" can belong to these given and yet unreflective moments of such a situation. If this examination were to attempt a detailed analysis of the ability to hear revelation, it would (as a "philosophical" investigation) have to examine both the "supernatural existential" (as given in an "experience of grace"), as well as the factual being affected by historical revelation. However, it remains restricted to the transcendence of the human spirit as a point of departure, of course in such a manner that this transcendence, at least in its beginnings, supersedes its own abstractness and therefore continually takes its place in concrete history.

[9] See above, note 8.

10

of an external word of revelation; or whether, in addition to human receptivity for this message (ascertainable by metaphysical anthropology) an interior elevation of man by grace is also an essential requirement, if the message that is heard is to become true theology, is a question, therefore, which remains outside the scope of our explicit consideration. This latter would obviously be just as useful a line of enquiry to clear up the whole problem of the relationship between theology and the philosophy of religion. It would, so to speak, be a path from above downwards (or better, from the whole to its parts), from the constitution of the believing man as determined by revelation and the light of faith (that is, by theology), to a metaphysical analysis of the *natural* man. This latter reveals the knowledge that man has if we exclude revelation and the light of faith, that is, from the whole to a residue, from theology to the philosophy of religion.[10] This line of examination would most likely lead automatically to a more accentuated exposition of the distinction between theology and the philosophy of religion. But at the moment we are following the reverse direction: from the natural, knowing man,[11] not to his theology of faith in its interior essence (which is impossible, according to what we have argued, because of the nature of theology), but certainly to an analysis of the possibility of perceiving the reality of the revelation of God as that Being which in fact alone constitutes man fundamentally in his fully developed essence. Obviously, whether or not the attempt at such an analysis can lead anywhere will appear only as we proceed with the attempt itself.

[10] See "Theologische Anthropologie," in *LThK* I, pp. 618-627.
[11] "Natural" is not to be taken here in the strictly theological sense as contrasting with the "elevation" of man through grace. Rather, it here refers to man insofar as he is "philosophically" conscious. The philosopher, for his part, can and indeed must take "everything" into consideration, and yet he can consider the historical, and whatever comes to him freely therein, as a liminal experience, since he thematizes the historical as the inescapable basic constitution of man and therefore continually releases man into his actually occurring history and destiny. In this sense, the philosopher too can be concerned with the grace allotted to man and with historical revelation, without thereby being a theologian.

11

(2) With that we come to the second difficulty which lies concealed within our definition of a scientific-theoretical question about the relation between two sciences, in the event of this definition being applied to the relation between theology and the philosophy of religion. The fundamental difficulty of defining this relation is underlined precisely when we bring together our provisional knowledge of these two sciences. We are to enquire after a single metaphysical foundation upon which both sciences are primarily constituted; and the relationship between the two is to be conceived by enquiring into their common root. But what can this common root be? The constitution of the philosophy of religion takes place in metaphysics —correctly regarded: *is* metaphysics itself. But can theology, too, be founded only upon metaphysics? Even if we understand this question only as just defined, that is, as a question concerning the *a priori* possibility of the capacity in man's nature to hear a supposed revelation proceeding from God, a paradox still persists. If metaphysics, as general ontology, has already laid in the knowledge of God the foundation of a philosophy of religion, that is, if it gives rise to judgments on the correct relationship of man to God, then does not all theology emerge too late? Theology, as the genuine listening to the revelation which has actually proceeded from God, and which is supposed first and foremost to define the correct relationship of man to God, thinks that it should be the first to decide certain things. But does not what we have just stated imply that these things have in fact, in every case, already been decided? Thus the philosophy of religion seems to have a metaphysical foundation such that, *a priori,* it takes up the place which theology might possibly fill. The one possible relationship between the two would lie, therefore, in this: that the one science abrogated the other, rendering it intrinsically impossible. At best, a theology of revelation seems to be but the more precise, historical elaboration of the relations between man and God, already defined by the philosophy of religion. But would theology not thereby be robbed of its intrinsic autonomy and the dignity that is independent of metaphysics? Furthermore, concrete revelation appears essentially as an historical process, not always and

12

everywhere to be encountered at will. In its object and its characteristic it is indissolubly attached to historical events in which the self-attesting word of God addresses itself to men. The philosophy of religion, however, seems to be essentially supra-temporal and transhistorical, for it purports to be metaphysics to which one is accustomed to apply these noble predicates. The philosophy of religion thus seems to institute a religion which is fundamentally independent of historical event;—a religion which all the time can be arrived at equally well from any point in the historical existence of any man;—a religion which is capable of being instituted ever anew, wherein every place is sacred country and every epoch the fullness of the time, because the spirit always and everywhere is able to attain to the "external ideas" of the true and the good and the beautiful.

What, then, have the philosophy of religion and theology to do with each other? How can they, in their duality, together and simultaneously be concerned and derived from a unified, common foundation, in a scientific-theoretical study? Our demand to have both initially constituted from one foundation within a single metaphysical problem seems from the outset to be absurd.

That this paradox can be resolved will only appear from our completed study. Were we to attempt to resolve the paradox first, we would in fact presuppose that we already know precisely what the philosophy of religion or theology really is. One thing, however, we can achieve: we may mark out negatively the place where a solution is possibly to be found, if such a place exists. The philosophy of religion, if it is to leave inviolate the interior autonomy and historicity of theology, must not be primarily the construction of natural religion; it cannot be allowed to trace lines that theology merely follows up and fills out more fully. The philosophy of religion must of itself point man to some possibility of revelation proceeding from God,—to a revelation, indeed, which occurs in history, if it occurs at all. Most certainly, the philosophy of religion may not have as its purpose, nor may it open up the possibility of, the institution of a religion that is contained within itself, and which then, subsequently, has either to be filled out or revoked by a theology of revelation. In terms of its own essence it must leave to the God who may conceivably reveal himself in history the institution and definition of religion, or at least place all of its propositions under the reservation of such a possibility. This, however, is equivalent to saying that metaphysics which is already philosophy of religion must be of such a kind as to recognize God as the free and the unknown, and to conceive of man as a being who is historical in terms of his transcendental subjectivity, and to direct man in his historicity to his own history, commanding him to seek, within his history, a possible revelation proceeding from this free, unknown God.[12] To the extent that such a metaphysics conceives God precisely as the absolute Unknown, as the One who cannot be unequivocally defined from below by human metaphysics, it does not presume to be able to make any *a priori* pre-judgment concerning the way in which this absolute, personal Unknown proposes to deal with men. Nor how and with whom this God desires and is able to reveal himself, or how he desires to initiate and prescribe the relationship between himself and man. In other words, it does not determine what religion must be. If, as genuine "natural" metaphysics, it does all this, then automatically it concedes first place to a possible theology.[13] Thereafter, it precedes it in such a way as to make room for

[12] This is of course not to say that the self-interpretation of man as something being, which *can* listen to a revelation possibly made real, *precedes* in all its aspects the *factual* hearing of such revelation. For an ability which by its own characteristics is relegated to history, constitutes itself fully only under the impact of the immediate historical event; otherwise the historical itself would not be linked closely to the building up of this ability, and would not, insofar as it achieved real ability in this respect, really and inescapably affect the essence of man himself; it would simply be added on after the fact, to a subjectivity already adequately constituted in its possibility. Rather, inasmuch as in the realistic consummation of historical power (here, in the actual hearing of pronounced revelation), the difference to its pure possibility (here, the ability to hear as such), is continually open, and actually becomes visible little by little in its full clarity, the line of questioning pursued here in the text is completely legitimate.

[13] See J. B. Metz, *Theologie und metaphysische Ordnung*, pp. 3f. Here, this openness of "natural" metaphysics towards a possible theology of revelation is enlarged upon on the basis of the concrete historical openness of the transcendental understanding of being of this system of metaphysics.

14

theology.[14] To the extent that such a metaphysics defines the nature of man as an essentially *historical* being who must pay heed to a revelation which may possibly proceed from God, the philosophy of religion becomes the sole possible man-centered foundation of theology. Thus the philosophy of religion and theology actually find a single metaphysical basis in one scientific-theoretical question; and so their mutual relationship is defined in this sense.

We may formulate the question regarding the relationship between the philosophy of religion and theology more precisely. We seek to elucidate one problem (which is a single metaphysical question): whether by metaphysical reflection man may legitimately define himself as possessing a nature capable of looking into his own history, hoping to see there a possible revelation from God who appears to him in human metaphysics as the essentially Unknown. If the answer is "Yes," we have arrived at the correct concept of the philosophy of religion. The sole possible pre-theological foundation of theology has been provided. The relationship between the philosophy of religion and theology has been defined so as to allow both to be understood in their individual distinctiveness, and also in terms of their common foundation.

And so our question concerning the relationship between these two sciences is ultimately a question concerning a metaphysical anthropology which has to conceive of man's nature in a twofold manner. (1) Man is a *spirit* standing essentially before the unknown God, before the absolute God whose "meaning" cannot be defined in terms of this world or of man. A positive and finally unequivocal relationship with him cannot be established from the human side, but only by God himself. Man himself must therefore always reckon with the possibility of a revelation from this God, indeed such revelation presents man to himself for the first time. The transcendental relationship which he

---

[14] This "making room" does not, of course, mean the disappearance of philosophy, since theology ultimately sets forth philosophy as its own and thus ever-present precondition for existence, and in this setting forth increasingly sets it free to itself. See J. B. Metz, *op. cit.,* pp. 8ff.

derives alone and uniquely from God's absolute good-pleasure is what constitutes his concrete nature. (2) Man is an *historical* being precisely as spirit, so that he is obliged to depend upon his history not only by virtue of his biological existence, but also as the foundation of his spiritual existence. It follows from this that man, by reason of his original nature, is from the very start already directed towards the historical contingency of a revelation, should it occur. Should God, of his free choice, wish not to reveal himself but to remain silent, man would attain the ultimate and highest self-perfection of his spiritual and religious existence by listening to the silence of God.[15]

For the present this is a sufficient definition of our problem. It supplies the basic foundation of such a metaphysical standpoint from which we are able to answer the explicit formulation of our subject.

---

[15] This is so because the abiding uncontrollability and never reflexively attainable remoteness of the entire human existence, in which the unique historicity of the human spirit and of its transcendental self-understanding is also apparent, ultimately can be grounded only in the unnameable divine freedom which inevitably reaches into that existence. The inexhaustible freedom of God in its (differentially experienceable) transcendental inescapability for man and his self-understanding is the grounding ground of the historicity of the human spirit.

2. THE SUBJECT
in Relation to Kindred Questions

In the first chapter we gained a preliminary conception of the general objective behind our search for the foundation of a philosophy of religion. In clarification of this question it ought now to be compared with other similar or contrasting questions. In this way we may expect our problem and our purpose to emerge even more clearly.

(1) First of all, let us try to place our subject in relation to the usual course of fundamental Catholic theology. Fundamental theology comprises the scientific substantiation of the fact of the revelation of God in Jesus Christ. Although the questions concerning the nature and function of fundamental theology have by no means all been answered within the framework of Catholic theology, and although the argument about them has, in fact, been once more set in motion during the years since the modernist crisis (as a result both of discussions with existentialist philosophy and evangelical theology, and discussions on the problem and idea of a Christian philosophy[1]), there can, however, be no doubt of the possibility and necessity of a rational foundation for faith ("foundation" or "reason" being used, admittedly, in a very special sense). The statements of the Church in the 19th century, and all those opposed to modernism and all immanentist apologetics, down to *Humani generis,* allow of no doubt on this point. Thus, in line with the *customary* routine of fundamental theology in its 19th-century form, the fact of the existence of a personal, supernatural God is first assumed to be demonstrated by special metaphysics (by

[1] See J. B. Metz, "Christliche Philosophie," in *LThK* II, pp. 1141-1147.

theologia naturalis or theodicy). Then fundamental theology itself demonstrates the possibility of a revelation on the part of God. That is, it is proved at least negatively and defensively that there are mysteries inaccessible to man on his own strength, which provide a possible subject of self-disclosure by God through revelation. Then it is deduced that it is materially and morally possible for God to reveal such mysteries to man, and that such a thing is suited to man, and in certain respects and under certain conditions is necessary. And finally it is expounded in the first part of fundamental theology that the God who reveals, on the one hand is able to impart knowledge of this mystery to a bearer of revelation through prophetic inspiration, and on the other hand can, by miracles, sufficiently convince the man to whom the revelation is addressed of the actual occurrence of such a revelation. Thereafter, in the second part, fundamental theology undertakes to prove that such a revelation has actually occurred in Jesus Christ, and that this revelation continues to be preserved and preached unaltered through the teaching office of the Catholic Church.

In this customary routine of fundamental theology there is one piece of conceptual foundation of faith that is scarcely, if ever, explicitly mentioned. This is that very question which has emerged from our present definition of the subject of our exercise. To begin with, in this fundamental theology the relation of the knowledge of God supplied by natural metaphysics to the possible content of revelation is as a rule only very superficially defined. It would appear that the revealed mysteries are added on to natural knowledge as a new piece of knowledge. It is true that in its innermost core at least the content of revelation is to be defined as *mystery* in the strict sense, that is, as a datum so inaccessible to man's mind that it can be known actually to exist only through the word imparted by God, and then, having been thus imparted, as incapable of positive scrutiny in its inner reality.[2] But this is not a sufficient explanation of the relationship between natural metaphysics and the knowledge that comes by

[2] For a more detailed presentation and critique, see "Ueber den Begriff des Geheimnisses in der katholischen Theologie," in *Schriften zur Theologie* IV, pp. 51-99.

18

faith. If at first it seemed as though revelation were nothing but the imparting by God to man of information of which he was hitherto ignorant, so that some new knowledge seemed to become attached to the previous knowledge in man, on the other hand it now seems that this description of the content of revelation as a *mysterium stricte dictum* once again tears apart these two elements of knowledge in such a manner as to threaten to make incomprehensible how such a mystery is at all conceivable in man. At the least it makes it incomprehensible how it can be the content of *his* knowledge, with which he is able to assume an interior relationship or an orientation, at least of the kind that would make him capable of receiving such revelation at all. In other words, the usual fundamental theology illumines but dimly how man on the one hand by virtue of his intellectual nature is able to become capable of receiving such an "extension" of his knowledge—how, that is, a place for this possible knowledge in man could be found in his natural essential equipment; and how on the other hand this knowledge itself is not already a fundamental, necessary fulfillment of his essential constitution. The mere assertion that because of this or that contingent cause or obstacle it is impossible for him on his own to attain such knowledge imparted by revelation does not resolve this uncertainty. And even if this impossibility is sought in the inner nature of the subject-matter that is accessible only through revelation, the information remains incomplete as long as it does not simultaneously become clear how it is that man stands receptive for such a subject-matter, in virtue of his own essential constitution, although the subject-matter is *in itself* inaccessible to him, in other words as long as the relationship between the content of revelation and human knowledge is not understood *in human terms* also.

This uncertainty also manifests at its most obvious, in that customary fundamental theology does not make explicitly clear why man, *a priori,* in terms of his essential structure, is disposed towards the fulfillment of his knowledge through free revelation, and through it alone. (By "disposed towards" we do not mean that man has a legal claim upon a revelation, but that man is under obligation to accept it if it is freely and gratuitously ad-

19

dressed to him.) It is usual to prove this disposition by the fact that, on the one hand, such a revelation has occurred, and on the other, that man by virtue of his general duty of obedience to God also owes him the duty of paying heed to his commands—in this case of accepting the divine revelation in faith. In one respect, however, the obligation to listen, the necessity of reckoning with the fact that God may possibly grant a revelation, ontologically precedes the actual giving of such a revelation. This presupposes the possibility, charging man himself with the task of preparing a foundation based on his need to listen. Such a foundation is supplied, however, only in the most general and externally formal way if derived exclusively from our quite general duty of obedience to God. It must also be basically and antecedently (that is, logically prior to proof through the actual occurrence of revelation) proved that the kind of demand upon the duty of obedience represented by belief in the revelation granted can be part of the way in which human obedience to God makes itself manifest. Moreover, this demand upon obedience belongs to these ways essentially and *a priori,* being at the same time previously recognizable as such by man. That is to say, it must be proved that attentiveness to a possible command from God which extends beyond the content of the commandments already promulgated through creation in the *lex naturalis* belongs *a priori* to the nature of man. Only if that sort of listening for God's command belongs to man's constitution can obedience to a command actually given represent a concrete possibility and duty for man. Only then will the pre-condition be created which makes effective an actual command of faith from God. This, however, is the very question with which we will have to grapple.

Furthermore, in fundamental theology we find little explicit discussion of the fact that man in virtue of his nature is directed to look into history.[3] It is still true, however, that before any

[3] This point of view is *internally* connected to the afore-mentioned. For it is only if man is relegated to history already *in* his ontological constitution, that is, if his "abilities" also are determined as types of his self-development, that he knows himself of his own accord, in the course of his self-development, to be absorbed by the uncontrollable in an approaching historical event, to be opened to it and to what it disposes in an

historical fact at all is proved (in fundamental theology, for example, the mission of Christ or his resurrection as the fundamental miracles assuring faith), the duty of man to busy himself with such historical truths must be explained in terms of his nature. Only when it can be demonstrated in a metaphysical anthropology that the foundation of man's spiritual existence in historical events (and hence the question about historical happenings) belong a priori to the nature of man and form part of his inescapable duties, do we find that a basis for the assumption of the proof of a specific historical fact and the difficulty of a rationalist and enlightened philosophy, such as Lessing's, can be basically resolved. This is, that for the substantiation of "necessary" truths (in other words, the establishment of the "existence" of the truths fundamental to the salvation of man) an historical fact may not be previously considered. Only if, in constructing his metaphysical and moral concepts (should these possess the necessary concreteness for "assurance of existence" [4]) man in virtue of his nature as man is obliged to turn towards history, is Lessing's view (still alive in any species of Enlightenment and Liberalism) shown to be fundamentally in error. This view, needless to say, affirms that historical truths can never be a reason for the construction and modification of metaphysical and moral concepts. Only thus do we finally arrive at a conquest of modern historical skepticism (insofar as such a thing is possible in the realm of thought) which, with its natural scientific and technical ideal of evidence, is doubtful of and indifferent to an historically founded structure of man's existence. It must be proved to such skepticism that an historical foundation of human existence is a priori absolutely unavoidable, and that the freedom which manifests itself in such a foundation provides no

---

"obedient" way, without this "obediently listening" openness taking on the meaning of "exigency" in the formal metaphysical sense, thereby lowering this disposing principle itself, of necessity, merely to the level of an obvious correlate to this "exigency." Inversely, the historicity of man is taken seriously only when man knows himself to be placed into an *intrinsically* indisposable situation (that is, not simply a factually haphazard one), if, finally, he comprehends himself as one existing in the unnameable sovereignly disposing freedom of God.

[4] See *Das Dynamische in der Kirche*, Freiburg, 1958, pp. 14-37, 74-148.

instance contradicting the empirical evidence of truth, but emanates from the nature of man and the specific object of knowledge that is required for the foundation of his existence.[5] In short, it forms part of a complete fundamental theology to prove man's basic reference to his history as the sole realm wherein he can come into his true nature. Thus we may assert that our subject forms that part of fundamental theology which in actual development is usually so sadly neglected, namely metaphysical anthropology of man as the one who listens in his *history* for a possible revelation from God. If we name the aptitude for something *potentia* (remembering that in our case we are not concerned with an aptitude which can lay claim to its objective as of right, but which can only be claimed by this object and freely called towards it in obedience), then we may designate this piece of fundamental theology, with which we ought now to busy ourselves, as the ontology of the *potentia oboedientialis* for the free revelation of God. In so formulating the subject, we must take care to note that we are not dealing with a *potentia oboedientialis* for supernatural *grace* as the ontological elevation of man to share in the life of God, but only with the *potentia oboedientialis* to hear a possible *speech* of God which, should it take place, takes place at least to begin with in the realm of his natural perception—that is, through historical experience and through the human concepts and words which go to make up this experience.[6]

[5] See J. B. Metz, "Entscheidung," in *Handbuch theologischer Grundbegriffe,* I, Munich, 1962, pp. 281-288, esp. 285ff.
[6] The distinction made between the *potentia oboedientialis* for word-revelation and that for grace does not imply, of course, that these two messages of God, and thus these two "potencies" related thereto, are adequately distinguishable in the last analysis. A hearing of the word of God as *divine* word, (and not just as a word somehow transiently originating through his agency) is possible only if the power of comprehension *a priori* needed for the genuinely human consummation of this hearing has itself been enlightened "divinely," by what we call "grace." Inversely, the imparting of grace itself is always of itself the basic mode of revelation itself, because grace as the self-revelation of God, the absolute Spirit, to the spirit and freedom of man, never resides in man as a merely objective, absolutely pre-conscious condition.

(2) Besides this, our subject can be pertinently related to another problem much discussed in Catholic theology and philosophy. This problem can clarify our subject, and vice versa. We have in mind the possibility of a *Christian* philosophy; and the usual question is whether and in what sense there can be such a thing, considering the relative independence of a philosophy worked out with the human means of natural reason. If this age-old question is not to become a battle over words upon a subject upon which all are fundamentally in agreement, we must affirm that the Christianity of a philosophy must also appear by the way it points beyond itself (while still remaining genuine, pure philosophy) and introducing man to the attitude of attentiveness to a revelation which may possibly proceed from God. It thus becomes a *praeparatio evangelii,* through its understanding of man as *naturaliter christianus,* as one who stands ready to receive a revelation. This term is not attached retrospectively to the concept of man's nature merely because a revelation has in fact been given, but because man from the start has been thus originally and finally metaphysically conceived. To provide a metaphysical anthropology thus understood is precisely the task we have set ourselves. We may therefore describe our task as the basic establishment of metaphysics as Christian in the above sense.

This is indeed an important essential feature of Christian philosophy.[7] It implies no obliteration of the boundaries between a philosophy that is relatively independent in aim and allied methods, and an equally independent theology. In the case before us philosophy will not attempt to do anything but philosophize. That precisely by so doing it will become a *praeparatio evangelii* and lead beyond itself and place man before the prob-

---

[7] This aspect of philosophy as Christian does not exhaust the entire problem of the possibility and essence of a "Christian" philosophy, however. For an overview of the problem, see J. B. Metz, "Christliche Philosophie," in *LThK* II, pp. 1141-1147. On the "Christian" nature of philosophy in the sense of a determination in terms of intellectual history, and on the related question of the place and rank of "Christian philosophy" in Western intellectual history, see J. B. Metz, *Christliche Anthropozentrik,* Munich, 1962, pp. 97ff., 132 ff.

lem of an historical encounter with God, will obviously appear only as it follows its course. But philosophy remains, even when doing this, pure philosophy, unless we assume that a thing loses its independence by being integrated in the service of a greater whole. Our concept of Christian philosophy implants the Christianity of the philosophy deeper than if the latter were seen merely in the role of preservation of philosophy from error, by revelation and theology and its enrichment by these two through the setting of new problems. On the one hand, the purely negatively operating preservation from error, which ought to be attributed to theology alone, is not an intrinsic requirement of philosophy. Certainly, in this way, it can be shown what is surely false, but philosophy has not thereby attained a knowledge of the truth according to a genuine philosophical conceptual structure. A fructifying and enrichment of philosophy through problems set by theology seems also to be a somewhat doubtful practice. Such a view seems too much to overlook the qualitative difference between theological and philosophical conceptual structure. In any case, such Christianity would signify but a retrospective baptism of philosophy. That philosophy is Christian in the specific and original sense which constitutes itself and hence man as *baptizable,* which by its own means has attained a state of readiness to be abrogated by a possible theology instituted by God (abrogated in the threefold sense which this word has for Hegel). Philosophy is suspended, that is to say, it does away with itself by working itself out in its own field and destroying its own title to be the final existential rationale of human existence. By its very necessary understanding of this task it places man in an attitude of listening for a message from God, and so dispenses with itself as the complete rationale of existence. It dispenses with itself by elevating itself to a higher plane; it reaches that higher plane by finding itself, as the constitution of the possibility of the reception of a revelation by man, fulfilled upon the higher place of a revelation that has actually occurred. It is suspended (or preserved) because the possibility of hearing a revelation is preserved in theology in its actually being heard, thus coming fully into its own for the first time, and therein having to be ever instituted anew. In short, if

24

philosophy understands itself as the ontology of a *potentia oboedientialis* for revelation, then its Christianity, that is, its true independence and original relatedness to theology, is thoroughly understood. This view of philosophy obviously does not deny that within philosophy there are problems in plenty which do not in themselves point so directly beyond philosophy, and which are therefore not directly relevant to theology. If, however, philosophy did not wish to hear, intrinsically and explicitly, this reference to theology, it would forthwith become either a highly academic, existentially indifferent affair. It would desire nothing more to do with the foundation of man's existence, or, if it still made this claim, it would be genuinely anti-Christian, because it would undertake to find a reason for human existence independently of the revelation of the living God. Whoever is familiar with the common scholastic textbooks of philosophy will already have gained the impression that the Christianity of philosophy in this sense has not always been a prominent characteristic, despite its orthodoxy and much stressed ecclesiasticism.

(3) In conclusion, let us clarify our subject by looking at it from a third angle. We are confronted by two basic types of Protestant philosophy of religion, ever recurring in manifold modifications, still alive today. For such Protestant philosophies of religion (it is of no consequence whether or not they explicitly declare themselves to be philosophies), *either* the content of religion, expressed in experience, cult, doctrine, and so forth is merely the objectification of what is already supplied by man himself by, perhaps, religious subjectivity (whether understood as value-experience, feeling of sheer dependence, as experience of historical existence as an ever new and fundamentally unobjectifiable call to decision, or some such thing); *or* this content is the word of the living God in such a form that it is the judgment of all that is finite and human (that is, utterly unexpected and incapable of expectation, before which what is human appears as absolute hiddenness, as contradiction, as sheer self-emptying of the God who reveals himself in and through all this hiddenness and finite contradiction of himself, and so intensely that God as revealer actually becomes the dialectically

25

necessary correlative of that which is radically ungodly in man, and is basically incapable of being revealed except as the judgment of God upon all that is finite). Thus God is either the inner meaning and the possibility of the world and the historical existence of man and no more, or the sheer contradiction of man and his world. From this it appears that these two types in the end coincide: "revelation" insofar as this word is still used at all is simply the necessary complement of the nature of man himself, with now this, now that sign. In the first type, the sign is positive: God is the meaning and possibility (of historical existence) of human existence, or else nothing; in the second type the sign is negative: God is the "No" spoken to man, or else nothing spoken at all.[8]

In contrast to all this the subject we have set ourselves becomes a double task. On the one hand, we must demonstrate the possibility of God's being able to reveal himself in such a way that this revelation is more than a mere objectification of man's religious neutrality. This presupposes that man in his "infinitude" is unable by his own capacities to anticipate and reach the absolute totality of truth. On the other hand, this demonstration must be carried out so as to make obvious to what extent man possesses a spiritual openness for such a revelation. It must become intelligible how he is able and at the same time obliged to approach such a revelation, without allowing its content to be anticipated in this openness. For this reason this openness does not appear as the dialectical complement of his infinitude either. And so our task is to demonstrate that the positive openness for a revelation which God may possibly give

[8] Of course it must be well noted here that the description of these two basic types of Protestant philosophy of religion is what the word implies: a "typification" which the present outline confronts initially, in order itself to achieve clarification through the comparison. The naming of concrete historical realizations of these two types has therefore consciously been avoided. For most actual systems are characteristically subject to many interpretations through their very nature, which does not admit a completely fair relegation into one or the other of the two types mentioned, which have at any rate been only indicated here, and not revealed in their complete extent. Besides, this schematic approach cannot claim to comprise the *whole* of Protestant philosophy of religion, not even in the indication of type.

(that is, theology) is part of the essential constitution of man without this revelation in its content becoming the mere objective complement of this openness, definable in terms of this same openness. In this fashion it must also become apparent that revelation can truly be heard, without being merely the formal "Yes" or "No" to man.

Through the definition of our subject in the first chapter, and through this comparison with related themes, our task would seem to have been sufficiently defined, insofar as this is possible at all at the start of our discussion. We see theology and the philosophy of religion and their reciprocal relationship from the standpoint of the philosophy of religion, that is, of metaphysics. This implies, as we have already stressed, that we can succeed in making evident the nature of revelational theology only to the extent that this is possible from this basis. Perhaps, in an age when, even in Catholic theology, too much skepticism about fundamental theology and about the rational foundation of faith is gaining ground, it is good to demonstrate that a properly understood philosophy of religion does not in the least violate the autonomy of theology. On the contrary, the want of such a philosophy in the end allows theology to turn into a theologically embroidered and fundamentally false philosophy. If theology, therefore, becomes independent in the wrong sense, so that it no longer bears any relationship to metaphysics (that is, to the nature of man disclosed in metaphysics), then theology is in danger of becoming, at least logically, nothing more than a "No" to man. For all its utterances, which still have to employ human language, can really be nothing but a sheer "No" to man, an exclusively negative reference to the divine which remains utterly unknown. Thus there could be no question of a real self-revelation of God to the whole man; or else such a positivist-fideistic theology would fall, all the more unprotected, a prey to the critically unverified philosophy of the age, thus once again bearing testimony to the inescapability of philosophical thinking within theology itself.

PART TWO

THE OPENNESS OF BEING
AND OF MAN

3. THE LUMINOSITY OF BEING

Through the manner in which we understand our subject the possibility emerges, not of speaking *about* the philosophy of religion, but of conceiving it as it is in itself, as we practice it. We do not wish to speak about it as actually present, but to demonstrate how it is originally constituted in itself.

All metaphysics, when not merely spoken about but actually practiced, is an arduous task. We need not be surprised, when we get down to work avoiding the use of imagination, if we are compelled to accept the strain of concepts or, to borrow Hegel's phrase, to realize that metaphysics is always concerned with things which we "always know and always have known." Metaphysics is not, as are the separate sciences, the discovery of something hitherto unknown, but is the methodical, reflective knowledge of that which one has always known. Only if one is prepared to keep quiet, to hold in check the eager concupiscence of one's subjectivity which always sets out intent upon collecting its dues, and let the object speak for itself, only then does it make sense to enquire what the philosophy of religion is, how it and theology are related, why and how true philosophy of religion in the final analysis is nothing other than the command to man to turn his ear towards his history to discover whether the word of God has been sounded there.

One thing must be noted. It is metaphysics we are practicing; and metaphysics is a *human* science. Thus it is constantly and essentially infected by that danger and darkness from which man's nature cannot be relieved. If an individual indulges in metaphysics, such metaphysics will of necessity be stamped with his own limitation and inadequacy. Such a state of affairs is all the more painful when such metaphysics undertakes in a certain sense to make room for a possible revelation, room for the divine, and for divine certainties, or in other words to assure itself by reflection of this divinely established state. We cannot avoid, but must reckon with the fact that as far as our mere thoughts are concerned we will make the vessel smaller than it has to be in order to contain the treasure of divine faith. At the same time, we must note that what we say is an attempt at a scientific conceptual understanding of the being of man as the subject of a possible faith, an attempt which remains open to question and which we maintain in a tentative and pre-scientific manner, and yet which as believers we already know assuredly and properly. Should anyone feel that he cannot subscribe to all that has been said, that is no proof that he may not be one who is able to listen to revelation and give the assent of his whole being to it. Such a statement would be only the invitation to make more explicit in a special new work of reflective metaphysics what he and we already live consciously and authentically in the concrete metaphysics of our own existence (a human existence which at bottom is nothing other than a listening to the message of God, eternal light and eternal life, an immersion in the depths of the living God, disclosed to us in grace).

On this condition we may now approach our specific and immediate task, which is to sketch the outlines of a metaphysical analytic of man with reference to the capacity to hear the word of God which is addressed to man as the revelation of the unknown God in allowing the history of man to appear. To put a question metaphysically, however, is to put it as a *question about being*. Every metaphysical question must somehow embrace the whole of metaphysics. That being so, it is obvious that we will set about our task only with the reservation that it must suffice to sketch in the broadest outlines of an ontology of man as the potential recipient of divine revelation. To attempt more is utterly impossible. At the same time, we must remember that such a course actually contradicts the inner nature of metaphysical work. Metaphysics as science is really only accomplished when what is already known is slowly and methodically unfolded in strictly conceptual work, that is, when man seeks to conceive metaphysics in concepts to which he is already accustomed in his being and action. But should we venture upon the abbreviated course that is forced upon us, and describe it as a metaphysical reflection, we are justified only because whenever it is appropriate we will appeal to the metaphysics of St. Thomas Aquinas.[1] What we cannot attempt, therefore, will be assumed to have been already accomplished by him and so presupposed to be demonstrable in his work. Nonetheless, our task will be no mere repetition of what St. Thomas once thought, because the aspect from which we view the basic features of his metaphysics, namely with the intention of arriving at an analytic of the being of man as that which has the capacity to hear a revelation, was not explicitly dealt with by St. Thomas.

Our intention is to produce an analytic of the being of man. Metaphysics is, however, the question about the being of that which is, in the way that it is. It is the question: What is the meaning of "being"? This is the way in which metaphysics has always been conceived and still is understood today, although under various disguises. Man in his thought or action can never halt at this or that point. He wants to know what every thing is, especially in the unity in which all is always present to him. He enquires into the ultimate reasons, into the final cause of all reality, and to the extent that he recognizes each separate thing as existing, and ever being brought face to face with himself in such knowledge, he enquires into the being of all that exists. He practices metaphysics. And even when he pauses or even deliberately declines to carry on enquiring, he still produces an answer to the question. He declares the question to be unresolvable or meaningless, thus answering it, saying that the being of that which exists is unimportant, empty of meaning, something looking out upon him from every thing which exists, and making him appear to be enquiring about nothing. Alternatively, man implicitly turns some particular existent thing into being itself—matter or business, the life-force or death and resignation. Whenever man surrenders his own existence utterly to some such existent thing, by this making absolute of one existent thing he declares it to be the center of all that sur-

[1] See the author's interpretation of Thomas Aquinas in *Spirit in the World*, New York and London, 1968.

rounds him and of all that he is, and everything else to be but supports and expressions of this one thing. In this fashion he declares what *he* understands and wants to understand by being, and how he interprets himself as an understanding of being. He is practicing metaphysics. Thus we are compelled to indulge in metaphysics because we are always doing it. We are compelled to ask: What is the "being" of that which is?

Of every question, however, we must ask: From what direction is the answer to come? What is the principle of a possible answer? The question which has no answer simply is no question. But if it calls for an answer then it already brings with it a certain background, an unambiguous foundation upon which it can and must be set and from which the answer must proceed. Otherwise, any answer would be correct, even the most arbitrary. A question to which an answer can be given at will is no longer a question, because if all answers are valid, each becomes inapplicable so that the question calls for no answer.

But where indeed is this general question of metaphysics about being to look for its answer? The source of the answer must not reside within the question if it is to be the foundation upon which the answer can take its stand. From whence, then, is the principle of an answer to the general question about being to be taken when it calls absolutely everything in question, even itself; when it enquires into the first cause, into being pure and simple? From these reflections it emerges that the point of departure for the answer to the general question about being can be nothing other than the question itself. The point of departure of metaphysics is thus the question: "What is the being of that which is itself?" It is this question in the necessity with which it is asked by man. For if the question were not presupposed to be asked actually and of necessity, the man who declined either to pose it or to recognize it as having been posed would have removed every source from which an answer might come, thus making the answer itself impossible.

If, therefore, the question about being itself is described as the self-sufficient starting point of metaphysics with regard to every metaphysical answer and statement, this is not so merely with regard to its content, but at least as much with regard to its actual and necessary existence in the enquiring man.[2] A meta-physical suspension of assent with regard to the *answer* about being is thus impossible, because the *question* about being perpetually and necessarily belongs to the existence of man. Hence man perpetually and necessarily himself proposes the question, and thus by inclusion also the answer to the problem of being, within his existence.

Of necessity, however (to return in more detail to the point that has already been discussed), the question about being is part of human existence, because it is a concomitant of every proposition that man thinks or utters. He would not be human if he did not so think and speak. Every statement is a statement about some specific existent thing and is made against the background of a previous although implicit knowledge of being in general. Every true proposition, every judgment and every deliberate act, is not just the synthesis of two concepts along with the claim that the synthesis is legitimate, but the reference of such a mental synthesis to a "thing in itself" which validates it and the objective synthesis which it copies. This opening up of the place of a "thing in itself" into which the subject-predicate synthesis of the proposition is installed, is nothing other than the antecedent knowledge of being in general. As such it is knowledge (understanding of being) that man exists, so that man does not somehow first of all have to be brought to being, but the understanding of being which is his already must be brought to itself in him. Correspondingly, for St. Thomas also the knowledge of being in general is not the *retrospective* occurrence of knowledge of each separate individual thing on its own, but of its antecedent cause (not of course in temporal priority). This statement obviously refers to the immediate and inexpressible, not to the reflex, understanding of being in general. Only in the reflective

---

[2] On the question of how this beginning of metaphysics can be formalized once again from the necessity of the existence-question in human existence, to the beginning from the necessity of the enquiry after the question, that is, how the unavoidable occurrence of the question *as such* in human existence always constitutes the beginning of metaphysics, see *Spirit in the World,* pp. 71f. Here it is also shown how this absolute beginning (which, in that it is called into question, presents itself anew— as a question) develops itself necessarily as a thematic existence-question.

knowledge of metaphysics does it become a perfected object of knowledge and thus amenable to concepts. In short, human thinking is always accompanied by an unexpressed knowledge of being as the condition of all knowledge of the existing individual. Accordingly, the question is always posed by inclusion. What is this being, the concomitant knowledge of which accompanies every cognitive and active association with the separate objects of knowledge and of action? Thus we see that the question about being occurs of necessity in human existence.

To the extent that this starting point of all metaphysical questioning is antecedently grasped as characterizing the being of man, it becomes obvious how all metaphysical enquiry into being in general is an enquiry into the being of that existent thing which must necessarily ask this question, that is, it is an enquiry about man. Human metaphysics is thus always an analytic of man. *The question about being and the question about man who enquires form an original and constantly whole unity.* At the same time this relationship is our guarantee that we are not averting our attention from man when we seem to become immersed in the most general metaphysics.

The question, which of necessity forms the sole starting point within our existence of metaphysics, has thus three aspects.

(1) We enquire about *being in general,* not in the sense of the aggregate of all the things that exist in their multiplicity and variety, but in the sense of enquiring into the being which is attributed as one and, at least analogically as itself, to each thing which exists.

(2) The question about being must be *asked.*

(3) We must enquire about being in such a way as to enquire about the being of a thing which exists, that is, *distinguishing between being and existing.*

That the problem of being does bear these three aspects requires no long discussion. We enquire about being in general, for by so doing metaphysics becomes distinguished from the separate sciences. The latter enquire into a particular sphere of existence and with a particular, limited reference to existence. Metaphysics enquires into all that is insofar as it exists, that is, into the being of that which is in general. This is a genuine *ques-*

tion. That is to say, what being is, is admittedly manifest and *known* already, but not *recognized.* In spite of its being known the question about being is no mere rhetorical question, but the question is asked because we are not yet consciously in possession of that which we enquire about. And in the end, in and through our enquiry, being and that which actually exists will become ever more distinct. This is the very thing which enables us to enquire about being. That which actually exists is always already known to us, because we are for ever having dealings with it and encountering it. But what the being of that which actually exists is, is not known to us. And so we pursue our enquiries. Conversely, the need to enquire demonstrates that we necessarily distinguish being and what actually exists.[3]

These three aspects of the question about being have to be subjected to a metaphysical analytic, in order to discover what they already contain by way of answer concerning the meaning of being and the nature of the enquirer himself, and finally, in order to disclose something about the problem set in this work, of the foundation of a philosophy of religion. Chapters 3, 4, and 5 will deal with the first aspect, Chapters 6-8 with the second aspect of the problem of being; Chapter 10 will then deal explicitly with the third aspect.

In the metaphysical enquiry into being we first of all enquire about being in general. That is to say, the nature of being is knowing and being known in an original unity, which we would like to designate the "being-present-to-itself" (integrity) of the "luminosity" (subjectivity, understanding of being) of the being of that which actually exists. This is the first proposition of a general ontology, as far as it concerns us here. The nature of man, however, is absolute receptivity for being in general, or in other words, man is spirit. This is the first of two propositions of a metaphysical anthropology insofar as we have to develop it

[3] The human question itself is the locus of the "ontological difference" mentioned here. This difference must not, therefore, be objectively misunderstood, as if only a difference of object were meant, which wants to consider "being" independently of the existence-question and the comprehension of being residing therein, simply as an isolated constituting factor of single beings, only conceptually generalized in the "abstraction" of single beings.

37

here. These two propositions must now be expounded and their meaning clarified in the following chapters, as consequences of the first aspect of the general question about being. This chapter and Chapter 4 seek an understanding of the first proposition, Chapter 5 of the second.

The nature of being is knowing and being known in their original unity. In other words, being present to itself, and self-luminosity. First, the question about the "being of that which is" already expresses a provisional knowledge about being in general, for nothing at all can be asked about the totally unknown. Thus some kind of knowledge is already affirmed and expressed in the question about the meaning of being. And because the question about being in general calls everything in question, the knowledge implied by the question cannot be known apart from itself as though it were something objectively different from what is asked, and added accidentally to it from outside. Being, under enquiry, in all its questionability, is still known being. For metaphysics especially, being is the alpha and the omega, the beginning and end of all questioning. If being, within the same scope and in all the aspects under which it is sought in metaphysics, is always something already known, then the basic knowability of the being [4] in virtue of which a thing exists is implicitly affirmed. A thing which is essentially unknowable in its being is a contradiction. Such a thing is enquired about inasmuch as the possibility or impossibility of its knowledge is called in question, and there would be no foundation for such a question, since we cannot ask about something utterly unrecognizable. Every question has already posited the subject of the question as something known. An utterly unrecognizable thing cannot be a known thing. The first metaphysical question, the most general question about being, already places the fundamental knowability of all existent things within their being. *Omne ens est verum.* A thing which is, and the possible object of

---

[4] Nothing is here prematurely decided about the essence of this "realizability." Its concept may not be brought into this sentence from the outside; it must rather be derived from the transcendental experience of the understanding of being itself. All other kinds of realizability are only derived *modi* of realizability, if the condition of being is the reason that makes possible all kinds of individual cognition.

38

a cognition, are one and the same, for the being of that which is, is *knowability*.

To say this is to affirm also that every thing which is, as the possible object of a cognition, possesses, in its own right and by virtue of its being (that is, *essentially*), an interior reference to a possible cognition, and so to a possible knowing subject. The knowability is affirmed as an *ontological* definition, in the thing which is itself. But if this interior reference of every existent thing to a possible cognition is an *a priori* and necessary proposition, it can be so only because the being of that which is and the knowing of it form an original *unity*. Otherwise, this reference of every existent thing in its own right to an act of knowledge could be at best only *de facto,* and not a definition of these existent things provided by the essence of their being. An essentially necessary relationship of the interdependence of two facts must ultimately rest upon an original unity of the two. For if the two were *originally* separate, that is, if in their origin they were not relative to one another, their interdependence could never be necessary, but at most *de facto,* accidental. *Non enim plura secundum se unitur*. The being of that which is and the knowledge thereof are thus interdependent, because originally they are one and the same in their cause. This is to affirm nothing less than that being as such, to the degree that it is being and appears as such (in the "ontological differential"), is knowing. This knowing in an authentic unity with being is knowledge of being [5] that results in knowing that the knower himself *is*. Being and knowledge form an original unity, that is to say, the cognitive reference to itself is part of the essence of the being of that which actually is. Conversely, the knowledge which belongs to the concept of the essence of being is the being-present-to-itself of being itself. In its original concept knowledge is self-possession, and any thing which is, possesses itself in the measure in which it *is* being. And so we arrive at the first proposition of our general ontology which is to be deduced from the first aspect of our general question about being. The essence of being is knowing and being known in an original

[5] From what has been said it is clear that "cognition *of* being" takes being to be both subject *and* object.

unity, which we call the (conscious) being-present-to-itself of being. Expressing this in terms of modern philosophy we would say: the being of that existent being which is self-illuminating. Being is illuminated in itself.

This brief deduction is now to be expanded first of all by reference to propositions in Thomist metaphysics, and then further clarified by the removal of a misunderstanding which might well arise over this proposition. This cautionary removal of misunderstanding will provide us with our first concept of the analogy of the concept of being.

Omne ens est verum: knowability is a transcendental definition of every thing which is.[6] Transcendentality is thus to be taken primarily in its scholastic sense of supracategoriality, and in this place particularly, in the sense that knowability is not, as it were, an attribute added to being from without, or merely its exterior relation to a cognition which is accidentally capable of grasping the relevant existent thing. It is to be taken in the sense that the knowability belongs interiorly and *a priori,* in terms of the existent being itself, to the grasping of its essence. It only explicitly declares what has been already affirmed, in being itself, as the horizon of its luminosity. According to the Thomist axiom, therefore, knowability, as the being of the thing which is, belongs to the basic constitution of every thing which is. Metaphysical irrationalism, that is, an irrationalism which not merely denies the possibility of access by this or that knowing subject to this or that existent thing (which withholds the logos of the thing) but, in specific spheres of being ("values," "life," or whatever names we give), utterly bars the way to any kind of logical conception, is thus excluded from the start from any Thomist metaphysics. *Quidquid enim esse potest, intelligi potest.*[7]

Even for a Thomist ontology, however, this proposition is but the door of entry to the more essential understanding of the original identity of being and knowing in the being present

[6] See *Spirit in the World,* pp. 80ff.
[7] *Cont. gent.* II, 98.

to itself. It is the luminosity of being for itself, to the extent that being can be attributed to a thing which is.[8]

For St. Thomas, the original and fundamental concept of being and hence of knowable reality, from which all other reality and all other existents are merely derivative, is actual, *esse,* or more unequivocally, it is the *esse actu.* This has to be enunciated in advance if the following propositions of St. Thomas are to be properly understood in their fundamental importance and application. St. Thomas, then, stresses the original unity of the knowable and its cognition, and this signifies more than a mere reciprocity between the two. *Intellectum et intelligibile oportet proportionata esse* (not merely proportionally related to each other, but also) *et unius generis:* they must derive *from a single origin.* St. Thomas supplies the logical reason for this: *Cum intellectus et intelligibile in actu sint unum,* because otherwise the *de facto* unity of knowable being and knowledge in the actual cognition could not be made comprehensible in its possibility.[9] For St. Thomas, being and knowing are thus *unius generis;* they arise from a single, unified root, from an original unity. Being is knowing *in itself,* and knowing is the being-present-to-itself of the being of a thing—that is, that which is necessarily contained in the constitution of being, its reflection back into itself, its subjectivity. In terms of this metaphysical basic concept of being and knowledge, St. Thomas also expounds individual acts of cognition. He rejects the common conception of the act of cognition as an encountering something, as an intentional reaching out towards externality. Knowing does not occur *per contactum intellectus ad rem.*[10] If knowing and

[8] This formulation ("attribution") indicates that in the present attempt, the precomprehension of "being" is not yet examined or formulated in an enquiry as to the more precise relationship between the "being" here in question and the "being" encountered by each individual, which we inevitably and appropriately call the "existent." We realize that this most difficult question in ontology cannot be sufficiently explained even within the scope of the considerations in the present volume, so that the subsequent sections on "analogy" are subject to the same limitations. See below, chapter 4, note 1.

[9] In *Met. provem.*

[10] *Cont. gent.* II, 98.

knowability are inner marks of being, then no individual, actual cognition can be grasped in its metaphysical essence if it is conceived as the reference of a knowing subject to an object that is different from himself—as "intentionality." To say the least, this cannot be the first point of departure for the metaphysical comprehension of the essence of an act of cognition. The initial starting point must rather be sought in the fact that being intrinsically is knowing and being known, that being is being-present-to-itself. *Intellectus in actu perfectio est intellectum in actu.*[11] In English: the perfect ontological reality of the intellect is the currently known thing. This proposition, as a proposition about essence, can be inverted. The knowable, in order to become currently known, must fundamentally be the ontological reality of the intellect itself. It would be a sheer misunderstanding of St. Thomas, and nothing but a sign of a cheap and superficial interpretation, scaling down the profound metaphysics of Aquinas to suit the mind of a moron, were we to understand the identity of knowing and known, expressed in this and other formulas, in the sense that a thing known, as such, must be known by a knowing subject, and that conversely a knowing subject, as such, must know something, so that in this sense both are one. *Perfectio,* in the proposition quoted, signifies, rather, an ontological reality of the intellect as of a thing which is. *Idem est intellectus et quod intelligitur.*[12] *Intellectum est perfectio intelligentis.*[13] *Ens est intelligibile et intelligens, inquantum est ens actu.*[14] For St. Thomas, thus, *species* does not mean some kind of "intentional image," but is an ontological perfecting of the spirit as a thing which is. Thus the problem of the object known distinct from the knowing subject is solved, but not by an appeal to the *species* as an "intentional image." For St. Thomas, this phrase conceals within itself the problem of how an ontological definition of a knowing subject, as a thing which is, can provide knowledge of the *species* and of the object that is distinct from the knowing subject, through the awareness of

[11] *Cont. gent.* II, 99.
[12] I, 87, ad 3.
[13] *Cont. gent.* II, 98.
[14] *In II Met.* 1, 1, n. 280.

42

this ontological definition. We do not have to go into this question in detail now. By this reference to the correct concept of the *species* in St. Thomas we intend merely to avert the danger of allowing a too hasty interpretation to bar the way to an understanding of the fact that the primary starting point of Thomist ontological and epistemological metaphysics is, in fact, the proposition that knowing, in its primary and original concept, is the being-present-to-itself of the being of the thing which is. Therefore, anything is known in the measure in which it demonstrates itself to be ontologically identical with the knowing subject.

When we try to summarize this understanding in the proposition: knowledge in its original essence is the being-present-to-itself, or the "subjectivity" of the being of the thing which is, we find a clear parallel in St. Thomas. What we have called "being-present-to-itself" corresponds to St. Thomas's *reditio subiecti in seipsum*. For St. Thomas, knowledge is a coming-into-itself of the knowing subject, that is, a being-present-to-itself. This already demonstrates how in St. Thomas the common conception of knowledge as a moving outwards towards the multiplicity of knowable things as a *spargi ad multa* is totally refuted.[15] Admittedly, if knowledge is ultimately a coming-to-oneself, the problem of how a knowing subject can know something distinct from itself is thereby surrendered to a Thomist metaphysics, and must be solved by it. The solution which we have still to reach in detail must, however, be arrived at so as not to disrupt this original insight into the essence of knowledge. That St. Thomas regards this coming-into-oneself, this being able-to-be-present-to-itself, as the fundamental conception of being, is evident also from the fact that in a key chapter of the *Summa Contra Gentiles* [16] he expressly graduates and measures out the degree of existentiality or potency of being, of "attributability of being" as we might say, according to the degree of possibility of its coming to itself, of its returning into itself. A thing which is, "has" being in the measure in which it possesses the possibility of such a *reditio in seipsum*.

[15] *Opusc.* 28, 1.
[16] *Cont. gent.* IV, 11.

We consider, therefore, that, within the scope of the possibilities here available, we have sufficiently demonstrated that in a Thomist ontology there is a real place for our first proposition of general ontology: the essence of the being of a thing which exists is knowing and being known in an original unity. This we have described as the being-present-to-itself of being, or the luminosity of being to itself as "subjectivity."

4. THE ANALOGY OF "HAVING BEING"

Before going any further with this study we must now examine an objection which is bound to arise immediately to this understanding of being. If being signifies the original unity of knowing and being known, if it is fundamental to the conception of being that it be "present-to-itself," then it would appear that there can be no existent thing that is not an *a priori* identity of knowing and being known. In disposing of this objection we cannot go into a discussion of the basic thesis of German Idealism, for this point of view cannot fully be criticized without constant reference back to its historical and actual philosophical development. In our context it is sufficient for us to explain and present the proposition about the original unity of knowledge and being at which we have arrived, so as to make clear that it has nothing whatsoever to do with pantheism or debased idealism of any sort—that is, with what normally goes by that title.

Our proposition emerged as pre-condition for the possibility of all things which exist being basically knowable in their being. We saw this knowability as implicitly affirmed in the primary metaphysical question about the meaning of that which is, "as such" and in general. For this reason our first proposition about the luminosity of the being of that which is must be capable of more precise formulation in terms of its source, in terms of the fact that man *enquires* about being. But enquiry can be rationally directed only to that place where there is not only some thing to be asked about (that is, where there is a fundamental recognizability in that which is questioned), but where also a problem exists concerning this very thing that is the object of the enquiry, in other words where a genuine distance separates

45

the enquirer and the object of enquiry. (This will be explained
more precisely later on.) Thus we can only enquire about being
if the question has not been already answered *a priori* and in all
respects by the ultimate knowledge of the object enquired about,
or if a question (and hence an answer in the genuine sense,
which always presupposes a genuine question) has not antecedently been made impossible through knowledge which, *a
priori,* utterly prevents a question from arising. The fact that
being was an object of enquiry would display being as being-
present-to-itself in an original unity of being and knowing. The
very asking of this question about being now seems once more
to nullify this definition. Why, indeed, must we enquire about
being if it already always is a being-present-to-itself, a being-
reflected-in-itself? If the enquirer asks about being he must "be"
being, because in the question he already knows being, and he
can only know of being (according to the first proposition of
our general ontology) to the extent that he himself is the thing
known. And yet, the enquirer "cannot be" the being about
which he enquires because otherwise, according to this very
proposition, he would have to be in unquestioning identity with
this very being about which he enquiries. To this extent the
existing enquiring thing which is not-being, in its identity is not
that being to which our first proposition of general ontology
directly applies. The manner of being which permits predication by the enquiring thing which is, is thus not the being itself,
simply and in every respect, to which our first proposition
straightforwardly applies. On the other hand, this enquiring thing
which is, must "possess" the being to which this proposition
applies, for it was acquired from the first metaphysical question
about that which is in general, that is, from the question which
includes the enquirer himself in his "having being." But with
this, the understanding of being to which our proposition refers
begins to waver. It reveals itself as something that cannot be
affirmed unequivocally, as something which cannot provide an
unambiguous statement concerning its content, that is, concerning being as being-present-to-itself, by a sheer undifferentiated
attribution of being to the thing which is, in the sense of sheer
levelling-down identity. Our first material insight, that being is

being-present-to-itself or self-luminosity, now becomes a formal thesis, that the *degree* of being-present-to-itself, of self-luminosity ("subjectivity"), corresponds to the manner of potency of being. This is the manner in which being is attributable as understanding of being to a thing which is, and in which, therefore, this thing which is "has" being. Conversely, the degree of "having being" manifests itself in the degree in which the appropriate thing which is, is able to turn back on itself, that is, in the degree in which it is possible for it to be reflected in itself, to be illumined by itself and in this sense to be present to itself. Our first metaphysical proposition applies, then, only under the proviso that the thing which is be present to itself in this sense, that it represent a unity of knowing and being known in that degree in which being is attributed to it. This attribution of being itself is an interiorly variable quantity. The starting point from which our first proposition was attained has also yielded the fact that this "attribution of being" is fundamentally not a fixed quantity, always and everywhere the same in meaning (to some extent not to be regarded as an unambiguous number), but as a concomitant function. Thus it emerges that "being," insofar as it displays itself as attributed to the individual thing which is, is interiorly unspecifiable in its most formal concept. In *this* sense the understanding of being is an *analogical* concept; and this analogy manifests itself in the sheerly analogical manner in which each and every thing which is, returns into itself, can be present to itself and therein is a "having being." [1]

---

[1] It is hesitantly and with much deliberation that we have chosen, in explicit assent of the author, the words "having-being" to formulate the concept of *analogia entis*. This concept remains in many ways unsatisfactory, not in the least as a simple coinage; it testifies to the fact once again that in the course of this work the "problem of being" cannot be completely analyzed and explained (see above, chapter 3, note 8). Nevertheless the formulation of the analogy as an analogy of "having-being" (and not simply the "analogy of being") should prevent any objectivistically hypothetical misunderstanding of being, that is, the "ontological difference" between being and being-ness, which easily tends to accompany analogical thought in considering this question. It is not "being" that is analogical, but rather the rising of the difference between "being" and "existent" in their relationship to each other, in their self-clarification, in the cognition of being, and in *this* sense in the "having-

This knowledge will still have to be applied in detail to man and to the primary and original object of his specifically human knowledge. This will become yet clearer when we deal with the second and third aspects of our problem of being.

If at this stage of development we want to refer back to Thomist ontology[2] we must point out that no matter how definite St. Thomas is about the material insight, that being signifies the being-present-to-itself of that which is, he is equally definite in preferring, in general, to express this basic idea of his epistemological and ontological metaphysics in the formal phrase at which we have just arrived, namely, in that formula which directly and immediately expresses the unfixable and analogical character of his concept of being: *eadem est dispositio rerum in esse sicut in veritate.*[3] *Unumquodque est cognoscibile in quantum est ens in actu* (and, following the principle *"idem est intellectus et intelligibile,"* we may add at once:) *unumquodque est intelligens et intelligibile, quod est idem, in quantum est ens actu.*[4] *Secundum quod aliquid est ens, secundum hoc est cognoscibile*[5] *et cognoscens,* as, once again we may add, by analogy. These and similar propositions in St. Thomas affirm nothing other than that, on the one hand, the concept of the "having being" of a thing which is is itself not a rigid concept which cannot be generally prescribed in a single unequivocal sense (that is, in a

---

being" of the existent. For being "is" not "something" "next to" or "above" the existent, but the existent as relationship to itself (and thereby as an "ontological difference" as well) as the state of self-clarification, as unity, (not take-it-as-you-will!) of cognition and recognition; or more precisely, being "is" the clarifying of the self-clarification of the existent, "is" the unifying force of the unity of the existent of cognition and recognition. God also in this sense may not be thought of as simply "being," but—as we will detail in what follows—as the existent possessing absolute "having-being" and thereby as the existent of pure and absolute self-clarification, pure and absolute relationship to self as the existent of the complete (and not discarded) "ontological difference" (see below, note 7; chapter 6, note 4 and *passim*). We hope that the following oft-repeated use of the concept "having-being" will bring to light little by little the ontological meaning we attempt to attribute to it.

[2] See *Spirit in the World,* pp. 84ff.

[3] I-II, 3, 7c.

[4] *In II Met.* 1, 1, n. 280.

[5] *In VII Met.* 1, 1, n. 1304.

specific manner of being-present-to-itself); and on the other hand, that the interior clarification and luminosity, the knowing itself and being known of the thing which is, vary exactly and correspondingly with the variability of this "having being." Because the concept of being is analogical, and this analogy is evident from the very first beginnings of an understanding of what being is, therefore the meaning of being thus discovered (the being-present-to-itself) is also analogical. Being-present-to-itself, reflection-in-itself, is already differentiated according to the particular thing which is that which is under scrutiny. Once again let us refer to the chapter already mentioned in the *Summa Contra Gentiles*,[6] in which St. Thomas expounds at length this inner modulation of the *reditio rei in seipsum* as the constitution of the separate "grades of being." All things strive to return to themselves, want to come to themselves, to take possession of themselves, because the "having being" which they desire comes to be in the measure in which they take possession *of themselves*. All activities, from the sheerly material to the innermost life of the Blessed Trinity, are but modulations of this one metaphysical theme, of the one meaning of being: self-possession, subjectivity. "Self-possession," however, is itself realized through a double phase: a flowing outwards, an exposition of its own essence from its own cause—an *emanatio*, and a withdrawing into itself of this essence, which has expressed itself in terms of its specific cause—which has, as it were, revealed itself. The more interior the two phases are with regard to the emanating and returning thing "which is," the more this thing is able to express itself, and in so doing, keeping itself to itself, the more the thing thus expressed can perceive itself, all the more does being display itself to itself as its own specific being-present-to-itself. Then St. Thomas goes through the separate grades of being; the material thing which is, expresses itself to some extent in its external activity; it shows what it is. But what is displayed, the appearance of its cause in its activity, does not belong to itself; in expressing its being it cannot be taken possession of by that which expresses. It acts only upon others; in reality it only shows

6 IV, 11.

other things what it is, and all the time remains hidden to itself. It does not illumine itself, but only gives out light for others. Not until we come to man does the expression of his specific essence in thought and action return for the first time to itself. In showing, by thought and deed, what he is, man knows about himself. He perceives and understands himself. We cannot here go into this sketch more fully. It must suffice to have shown that in St. Thomas, too, the meaning of being as being-present-to-oneself, as luminosity, is an unfixed, analogical concept that is for ever inwardly modulating itself, one that reveals itself as such in the very place where being displays its essence as being-present-to-itself.

That is enough, at least provisionally, to allow us to ward off a pantheistic interpretation of our first metaphysical proposition. Being is knowing. True, but only in that measure in which a thing is, is there a "having being." And because this "having being" represents itself in an analogical concept (analogical for the same reasons as lie behind this first proposition), hence not every thing which is, is a "knowing" in the same sense and in the same measure. Not everything that is, is in the same sense "true," in the same sense a "having being." Hence it is possible to think of (even to affirm the contingency of) a thing which exists and in the way it exists as not a "having being" simply in the mode of absolute identity, and therefore is not an inner factor of a cognition of "absolute consciousness" either. The only thing which is that is an absolute "having being" or an identity of the thing which is with its being as a being-present-itself, is the "pure being" [7] in which the connotation of the concept of being itself is perfectly realized. In this case of absolute identity no further

[7] When God is here designated as "pure being," it is meant in the sense that God is the existent of absolute "having-being" and therefore pure self-clarification. The absolute identity of God may not be thought of as a lifeless indifference of that "being" with itself, which has always been an open question in our concern with the problem of transcendental being; rather it must be thought of as the "ontological identity" of absolute "having-being," in which at the same time the "ontological difference" is perfected, in which, then, the existent relates "absolutely" to itself, stands totally before itself (see below, note 1). This must always be kept under consideration when, in what follows, we discuss God as "pure being," as "absolute being," as "infinite being."

50

questioning is possible. For that which is in its very existence is "having being" pure and simple, possesses, *a priori* in absolute identity and thus with pure luminosity, that about which it would have to enquire, namely, being in general. The question is thus answered by a knowledge that has no questions to ask. It is the νόησις νοήσεως. But because not only asking questions about but also being in doubt about being is part of the basic constitution of man (because man must *ask questions*), man is therefore not absolute consciousness, but *finite* spirit. In his metaphysical question it is not absolute consciousness that is manifest; this does not emerge in man, not even in his transcendental consciousness; but what does emerge out of his need to enquire into being is the finitude of his spirit. It appears, however, in such a way as to show that being is being-present-to-itself. That being is luminosity, the original unity of knowing and being known. But we are already anticipating the study of the second half of the first aspect (which will have to deal with man) and the second and third aspects of our problem of being, which is the starting point of all our questioning about the ontology of the human subject of a possible revelation on the part of the absolute God.

By these reflections on the meaning of being and on the analogy of "having being" have we not strayed into realms very far distant from the sphere of our proper interest? Not at all; we are now right at the heart of real philosophy of religion, insofar as this is to be our foundation of a possible revelation by God, for if revelation is to be the disclosure of the absolute, by itself, to the finite spirit, then two things are presupposed. First, that all that is, can fundamentally be turned into a "true" speech, into an information, addressed to the mind. Only on this condition can the possibility of the imparting of facts that are hidden in God be considered at all. This, at the very minimum, is what we mean by revelation. And this is what we have been discussing. The ultimate presupposition for God in his divinity, communicating to men through speech, that is, through the Word, is the ultimate unity of being and knowing.[8] Only if the being of that which is, is "logos" from the very start, can the

[8] This is always meant to be taken in its unity with that which we call "grace" in theological terms.

51

incarnate Logos utter in words what lies hidden in the depths of God. Only if these depths are not a dark urge and chaotic primal cause, not blind caprice, but eternal light (even if inaccessible to man in his own strength), can the Word be the bearer of all grace and truth. And that, indeed, is all that we have so far affirmed, not in mere poetic phrases, but as far as possible clearly and logically through conceptual effort. We have been engaged in the philosophy of religion in its original sense.

5. MAN AS SPIRIT

The second presupposition for the possibility of revelation is this: man must possess an openness for the self-utterance of the one who possesses being absolutely through the luminous Word. This openness is the *a priori* presupposition for the possibility of hearing such a Word. This determines our next task: to deduce from the first aspect of our general question about being what can be said concerning a metaphysical anthropology of man as a thing which is and who is *a priori* open towards a possible revelation.

When, at the beginning of Chapter 3, we specified the three aspects of the general problem of being, the first was said to be an enquiry into being in general. As this question is to be studied, not just in its content, but also in terms of the necessity with which it is affirmed in man's existence, any analytic of the question is simultaneously an analytic of the existent thing which poses the question about being. And so it is proper to make explicit what the first aspect of this question implies for a metaphysical *anthropology*. It implies that man is absolute openness to being in general, or, in a word, that man is spirit. Transcendentality with regard to being in general is the basic constitution of man. And so we enunciate the first proposition of our metaphysical anthropology. The justification and meaning of this proposition have now to be expounded.

Once again we must proceed from the most general question of metaphysics: what is the being of that which is, specifically and in general? This question, as we have reiterated, arises of necessity in human existence, so that the answer, too, which is found within this question, must be affirmed with equal necessity. The necessity of the general problem of being in human existence was explained earlier, by saying that it is a concomitant of all human thought and action. We must now expound this reasoning in more detail, in order to make clear how the knowledge of being in general, which is already given with the question, is related to that human thought, speech, and action, which make up man's existence in general.

Man lives within a world of existent things which are the objects of his activity. Man is not simply one of the goods and chattels at the disposal of his environment, but lives in a world over against which he takes up his stance and from which he differentiates himself in thought and deed. He judges the things which he uses, and as he uses them. He does not simply come into some sort of cognitive contact with the things of his world, as it may be supposed the animals do. But in judgment, he distinguishes himself from the thing he knows. He turns the environment of his physical-biological life into the object of his activity, into his world. He not only knows and feels his environment, but judges it, thus constituting it for the first time as a *world*. He is the subject that stands over against an object. His knowing is not just a becoming one with another thing in a neutral center between a within and a without, between subject and object, as will yet have to be explained of sense-perception. But in the comprehending reaching out to things, man as subject returns so completely to himself, as that which is differentiated from what he went out to grasp, from the world, that in himself he is a subject distinguishable from the thing known, this thing which is "other" and stands apart from him. Thereby his experience through sense becomes objective knowledge in thought. St. Thomas calls this return to oneself as subject, in a self-luminous antithesis of the sensibly experienced object, the *reditio completa subjecti in seipsum,* its subjectivity. In this perfect return to itself St. Thomas sees the distinctive attribute of the spirit in contrast to all that is sub-spiritual. This subsistence of man in itself manifests itself in all human events to the extent that they are truly human. It displays itself in judgment [1];

[1] For a more precise presentation of this transcendental judgment-analysis, which understands judgment as the post-carrying-out of that

for in every judgment there takes place the reference of a known something to an object, of a predicate to a subject. And insofar as every judgment presents a claim to truth, it has in mind, as the object of its predication, something that is itself independent of the passing of the judgment. It has in mind the object in its "in-itselfness." In so doing, the one who judges sets up the object of his judgment as something different from and independent of his judgment (at least in an ideal "in itself"), and thus differentiating himself from the object, places himself apart from it. In this way the one who judges comprehends himself in this separation from the object of his judgment. In every judgment he comprehends himself as a subject that subsists in itself. That is, he comprehends himself in his subjectivity. And insofar as man's thought is always expressed in judgments (for man always thinks something about something, that is, judges), this process which we have tried to describe takes place in all his thinking. The subsisting-in-itself manifests itself further in all human *activity,* insofar as this is specifically human. Human action is free. Freedom, however, is *a priori* conceivable only where the actor occupies a position that is independent of the position of that upon which he acts. By accomplishing his perfect return into himself through his thought-judgment (thus gaining a stance that is opposed to and independent of the known object), man is able to act freely upon it, as one who is freer than it. Conversely, the fact that man is able to act freely upon the things in his world is a pointer to this conscious "subsisting-in-himselfness" of man in his cognitive activity. This conscious "subsisting-in-himselfness" is thus part of the essential constitution of man, to which he testifies and which he affirms, in every contingency of human existence.

What has been said in general of human thought and action obviously applies also to all thought-judgments, which occur in the problem of being in all its ramifications. This question about that which is in general also posits that which is, about which we enquire, that is, as a thing being-in-itself, to which the desired answer is supposed to apply. And it is supposed to apply as to

---

"judgment," which is man himself, see *Spirit in the World,* pp. 129-242, esp. 173ff.

something antithetical to and independent of the question. Within the question about the being of that which is specifically and in general, a judgment is contained: it is a thing which is. This judgment is, however, but the most general and formal expression for that objectivication of an object within human thought and action, in which the conscious subsisting-in-itself expresses itself. This, then, is always expressed even in the most general enquiry into being. We are justified, therefore, in posing the question about the ultimate cause of this conscious subsisting-in-itself with reference also to the most general question about being. The problem of being, thus outlined, is, however, only the actualizing consequence of that original judging which is present as the ontological differential in the understanding of being as the permanent cause of every individual judgment. So also, *in this manner,* is the problem of being systematized as a judgment.

There now emerges the question about the ultimate cause of the possibility of man, in his subsisting-in-himself, taking up a position distinct from the things he handles in conscious thought-judgment. How must this comprehension of things by man (in knowledge and action) come about (the terms of the concept of knowledge that we have already gained always includes union) so that it does not signify being comprehended in turn by the things with which man becomes one through knowledge? How does this consist in judgment and freedom, in a conscious subsisting-in-himself? What is the *a priori* transcendental condition for the possibility of this subjectivity? The answer to this question will provide the starting point from which we may expound and clarify the first proposition of our metaphysical anthropology which we have already stated. To the extent that this subsisting-in-himself is revealed even in the first question about being as a necessity of human existence, the question about the condition for the possibility of this subsisting-in-himself is also a further stage in the analysis of what is implicitly concomitantly affirmed in this starting point of all metaphysical enquiry.

Our question about the nature of man has so far led to a preparatory, and as yet fairly obvious, insight. Man is that existent thing which is able to perfect itself as a *reditio completa.* This seems a very meager result for so many words. But it has been necessary to stress thoroughly this apparently obvious fact, because it will provide the starting point for the proof and understanding of the statement that man is spirit.

In every judgment a thing which is actually, is affirmed in a specific individuality: this is such-and-such a thing. To a certain extent this is the most general form of judgment. This is seen in action also, for there, too, man is always dealing with something that is precisely of a particular and specific sort. The taking hold of an individual object as a thing of this or that specific sort is nothing else than the comprehension of the particular under a general concept. It is to this which thought and action is directed. The particular, presented ultimately in and through the senses, is brought to the level of concept. This taking hold of the particular in concepts (the knowledge of the object as one out of the many, expressed by the predicate of a sentence) is but the other side of that which we have called the conscious subsisting-in-himself of the knowing human subject. Precisely by knowing something about something, by being able to apply its general concept to an object present, the one who knows conceptually separates himself from this object present as from his object. He thus attains his conscious subsisting-in-himself. The question as to the ultimate cause of the possibility of subsisting-in-oneself is thus identical with the ultimate cause, with the condition of the possibility of putting the individual case that is given in sense-perception into concepts, of grasping the universal in the particular.

In Thomist epistemology the catch-word for this process is "abstraction." By abstraction the universal is grasped in the particular, in the individual case, whereby a condition of possibility of judgment and thus the possibility of conscious subsisting-in-oneself is provided. Hence, seeking to understand the condition for the possibility of this subsisting-in-oneself, we must ask how and for what reason the possibility of the abstraction is to be comprehended. To *abstract* is to *loosen away from.* Abstraction is thus the recognition of the detachability of the "thisness" that is given in sense-perception, abstraction from the individual case in which this "thisness" is concretely contained.

The knowledge gained is that this abstraction does not belong to the essence of this particular thing which is realized in just this particular and in no other. Abstraction is thus the recognition of the non-restriction of the "thisness" that is given in the particular in this sense. It is also grasped as a possible determination of other particulars. The "thisness" (the *forma* or *quidditas* in scholastic terminology) is grasped as a determination which fundamentally extends farther than just to this particular case, in which it appears and in which it is known through the senses.

And so arises the question about the transcendental condition for the possibility of the knowing subject recognizing this non-restriction of the "thisness," in spite of its being experienced only in a specific case. We are seeking for the *transcendental* condition for the possibility of this situation, that is, for such a condition as must be attached to the knowing subject prior to particular knowledge and abstraction, as the antecedent condition of its possibility. In scholastic terms: we ask about the inner essence of the *capacity* to abstract. Because this capacity is also called *intellectus agens* in Thomist terminology, we may finally define our question as an enquiry into the essence of the *intellectus agens*.

Because the definition of quiddity ("thisness") is first of all given as narrowed down upon the particular sensibly perceived thing, the grasping of the non-restriction of this definition as such must take place by its restriction through the particular thing being grasped. For if the restriction as such and as affected by the "thisness" of the particular thing is experienced, the non-restriction of the quiddity as such is thereby also grasped. A limit is experienced in this direction, however (and that always signifies more than merely that it is actually present), when the "thisness" is experienced as an obstacle to any advance beyond itself. That is to say, applying this to our question: the restriction of the quiddity experienced through the senses, to the particular given by and through the senses (which restriction is made known as grasped by the non-restriction that is an intrinsic attribute of the quiddity), becomes known, in the reaching out of the act whereby the individual sense-object is seen prior to this grasping, to be *more* than just this particular thing.[2] This *"more"* obviously cannot be an individual object of the same sort as the one, the abstractive knowledge of which is supposed to have made this "more" possible. Were it so, the same question would begin all over again. This "more" can only be that being already mentioned as the fundamental cause of possible objects and of their encounter. In particular, this "more" is itself never one object among others, but the opening up of the absolute breadth of possible objectivity in general, and thus by virtue of the fact that consciousness grasps its particular object in a pre-concept of being (as we wish to designate this process of reaching out to grasp the "more") and hence of the absolute breadth of its possible objects. In each particular cognition it always reaches out beyond the particular object, and thus grasps it, not just as its unrelated, dead "thisness," but in its limitation and reference to the totality of all possible objects. This is because consciousness, by being close to the particular in order to know it, also always reached out beyond the particular as such.[3] The pre-concept is the condition for the possibility of the universal concept, of the abstraction which in turn is what makes possible the objectification of the datum of sense perception and so of conscious subsisting-in-oneself.

What we mean by the pre-concept must be further clarified. It is a *capacity* of dynamic self-movement[4] of the spirit, given *a priori* with human nature, directed towards all possible objects. It is a movement in which the particular object is, as it were,

[2] This "pre-concept" must of course always be considered as not removing the liminal experience, since the limit is at the same time the lasting and ever-present condition upon which depends the possibility of the "pre-concept" itself. This alone suffices to make it clear that the "pre-concept" in the *modus* of a particular abstraction, represents this "more," in the light of which abstraction the "pre-conceiving" human always knows himself to be relegated back to his finiteness.

[3] "Beyond" in the sense of the designation "liminal experience" mentioned in note 2, above.

[4] This "self-movement" of the human spirit does not mean that being is merely the static-objective condition that rests in itself, towards which the spirit is directed "from outside"; here, being is rather revealed as that encompassing whole which draws to itself this *self*-movement of the spirit. See H. Overhage and Karl Rahner, *Das Problem der Hominisation*, Freiburg, 1961, pp. 43ff.

grasped as an individual factor of this movement towards a goal, and so consciously grasped in a pre-view of this absolute breadth of the knowable. Through this pre-concept the particular is always, as it were, recognized under the horizon of the absolute ideal of knowledge. Hence it has always already been set within the conscious sphere of the totality of knowable things. Hence, too, it is always already known as not completely filling up this sphere, that is, as limited. Insofar as it is seen to be limited, the essential definition will be understood in itself as wider, as relatively unlimited—that is, it is abstracted. For this to be possible, this pre-concept and the breadth of the knowable that is disclosed through it, must be known in a manner that can be more precisely defined. It must be known, obviously, only in and by the grasping of the particular object, for the knowledge of which it appears as the presupposed condition of possibility. The pre-concept is the conscious opening up of the horizon within which the particular object of human knowledge becomes known.

We can describe the essence of this pre-concept more precisely by defining more exactly the breadth of this horizon which it opens up and into which it sets the particular object of knowledge. First of all, it is indeed enlightening, as we observed in passing, that this object to which the pre-concept is directed cannot be an object of a kind such that, the abstractive and objectifying knowledge of which it makes possible. Such an object would itself be knowable only in such a pre-concept. Likewise, although the pre-concept is conscious (otherwise it would have no meaning at all for our enquiry), nonetheless it is not in itself an act of cognition, but a factor in an act of cognition, which is specifically directed towards a particular object. However, the pre-concept must be described so as to allow it to be conceived (if not exactly affirmed) as knowledge *per se,* even if it is only the condition for the possibility of knowledge. This is because we are always compelled to imagine such cognitive reaching out to what is to be known as if it were a typical human cognition. But if we are obliged to think of the pre-concept itself as a cognition, this description in turn can only be given in such a way as to indicate the *object* of such a cognition. In this sense, therefore, we ask what the object of the pre-concept is. In anticipation we have already said that it is being and thus the totality of the possible objects of human knowledge. But how can we specify this totality more exactly? [5] What is the absolute totality of all possible objects of knowledge within the horizon of which the particular object is grasped? Or (if we cautiously wish to avoid speaking of the *totality* of all objects of knowledge), what is the transcendental reference for human pre-conceptual cognition, when it is grasping its particular object?

To the question put in this way, three basic types of possible answer suggest themselves. The interpretation of the pre-concept as related to the "negation" implied in the transcendental experience of limitation results in: (1) a turning of this "negation" into the absolute "nothing" as the genuine "truth" of the cognizand, and which is to be ever discovered afresh; (2) a constant concealment of this "negation" as that which is fundamentally outside knowledge; and finally: (3) by this transcendental experience of the "negation" being expounded as the mode in which absolute reality makes itself present by perpetually withdrawing and precisely *thus* drawing the intellect upon itself. [6]

It is obviously impossible, within the scope of this work, to treat this problem and its solutions in a manner comparable with its fundamental importance. We must be content with a brief sketch of the scholastic answer to the question, and to see how it corresponds to the third basic type mentioned above. Human cognition is related, at least at first, to that which is, and thus to *affirmation*. To the extent, therefore, that knowledge of the finitude of the immediately given object of a cognition can be explained in terms of an affirmative knowledge (and thus in terms of a pre-concept which is related to affirmation, to being and not to non-being), to the same extent the transcend-

[5] The question posed herewith concerning the "meaning of wholeness of possible objects" at the same time permits a closer defining of the "meaning of being," without it becoming necessary to identify both questions which would suggest the necessity of adequate answer to the existence question.

[6] Here also we consciously forego mentioning concrete historical examples for these three basic types (see chapter 2, note 8).

ence cannot and may not be interpreted as a transcendence correlative to non-being. Further, a transcendence relative to non-being was not indicated as the pre-condition for the possibility of experiencing the inner finitude of the immediately given, present, and existent thing. Now because the pre-concept relative to "more" is the particular object, it represents a sufficient and clear condition of the possibility of negation, of the transcendental experience of nothing (of no-thing) and thus of the knowledge of the finitude of the immediately perceived objective particular. Non-being does not precede negation, but the pre-concept relative to the unlimited is in itself already the negation of the finite, to the extent that, as condition for the possibility of its cognition, and through its rising above the finite, it reveals, *eo ipso,* its finitude. The affirmation of the thing that is in itself unlimited is therefore the possibility for negation, and not the other way around. Thus we are not required to assume a transcendence relation to non-being, which, preceding all negation and providing its foundation, would have to disclose the finitude of an existent thing for the first time. Positive unlimitation of the transcendental horizon of human knowledge automatically displays the finitude of all that does not fill up this horizon. That is, it does not destroy non-being, but the infinitude of being to which the preconcept is correlated discloses the finitude of all that is immediately present to sense. Thus *to begin with* we can deal only with the question whether the "more" of the preconcept denotes merely a relative unlimitation, or the intrinsically pure unlimitation of being in such a fashion that this preconcept opens up a sphere beyond that of space-time sense-perception. Our first assumption contains a contradiction, though not in the pure content of the concept itself, as though the totality of the objects of human knowledge on the one hand were set in immediate conceptual contradiction to "finite" on the other hand. The contradiction is between the setting of this assumption and its content. The recognition of the inner finitude of the totality of the objects of human knowledge certainly does demand a pre-concept that reaches out beyond this finitude, in order that this inner finitude can be grasped as such and not merely recognized as factually present. This pre-concept, reaching beyond the inner finitude of the human sphere of objects, beyond the level of sense perception (the pre-concept which alone can name a datum of this finitude as such) would have therefore to be directed towards non-being, because by pre-supposition it may not be directed to the infinitude of being. However, such a pre-concept relative to non-being has just been exposed as an unrealizable assumption. The pre-concept that is the transcendental condition for the possibility of an objectively possessed object, and thus of the subsisting-in-himself of man, is a pre-concept relative to being that is unlimited in itself. Thus the ultimate question that remains is whether this unlimited being can be and *must* be knowable, or whether this positivity may be present to the intellect *only* by constantly turning away from it. Because this question is unavoidable, it has already been implicitly answered in the first supposition, for the complete denial of a question does not void the knowability of the material about which we enquire. The positive answer is not intended to obscure the specific insubstantiality of that which is positively experienced in the recognition of non-being in the experience of limitation. The intention is to make this present in terms of its hostile intractability towards the *whole* man who always lives in concrete fulfillment. To the extent that our first and most general question about being is only the formalized expression for *every* judgment contained in all thought and action, it can be said of that judgment that in it the pre-concept is made concerning being pure and simple in its unlimitation. To the extent that judgment and free action are necessarily part of man's existence, the pre-concept of being pure and simple in its own intrinsically proper infinitude is part of the fundamental constitution of human existence.

God is posited, too, with the same necessity as this pre-concept. He is the thing of which is affirmed absolute "having existence." It is true that the pre-concept does not present God immediately as object of the intellect, because the pre-concept, as condition for the possibility of objective knowledge, does not present any object at all along with itself. But in this pre-concept (as the necessary and ever already actualized condition for every human cognition and every human action) the existence of an existent thing of absolute "having being" (that is, of God) has already been affirmed, if not presented. In the pre-concept the cause of his specific possibility is unknowingly affirmed. In the pre-concept, being, as the cause of this possibility, discloses itself in such a way that it is attributed to the thing which is. It does this not merely remotely (as in the occurrence of the pre-concept itself, that is, in unfulfilled ontological differential), but it displays the absolute "having being" of the thing which is, as the cause of all existential future, because the positive character of being makes the nothing of the unfulfilled ontological differential possible, and not the other way around. And so we may state: the pre-concept is directed towards God. It does not aim directly at God, so as to present absolute being in its specific self, immediately and objectively. It does not make itself specifically an immediate datum. The pre-concept aims at the absolute being of God in the sense that the *esse absolutum* is always fundamentally affirmed through the former's basic unlimited breadth. This is no purely *a priori* proof of the existence of God, for the pre-concept and its breadth declare itself as an actual and necessary condition for all knowledge only through the *a posteriori* perception of a real existent thing. It is the necessary condition for the perception of such an existent thing. Thus our version of the knowledge of God is only the epistemological expression of the real-ontological formulation of the traditional proof of God's existence. Instead of saying: the finite existent thing, affirmed as *actually* there, requires, as condition for its existence, the existence of the infinite being of God, we merely say (meaning in fact the same thing): the *affirmation* of the actual finitude of an existent requires, as condition for its possibility, the affirmation of the existence of an *esse absolutum,* which takes place implicitly already in the pre-concept of being in general, through which the limitation of the finite existent is for the first time recognized as such.

It must be repeated that it is unfortunately impossible to demonstrate in detail the traditional Thomist formulation of the thought which we have so far developed.[7] We would have to

[7] See *Spirit in the World,* pp. 192ff.

speak of the connection between the *reditio completa subiecti in seipsum,* which is accomplished by the human intellect in all its thinking, and the *abstractio,* that is, of the connection between that which we have called man's subsisting-in-himself and the grasping of the objectivity of the particular sense-datum through its concept. Proceeding from this we would then have to explain what the faculty of *abstractio,* of the *intellectus agens,* is. Then it would in fact appear as the faculty of the pre-concept of the *esse.* The *intellectus agens* is the *"lumen"* which informs the sense-datum, that is, which introduces it into the realm of being in general, thus allowing its participation in being in general to be recognized. Conversely, this "light" (in its unrestricted breadth, which is the very knowledge of being in general), by the thus constituted *intelligibile actu,* comes into man's consciousness. Against this background we would then be able to grasp the true and deep meaning of the apparently simple statement, that the formal object of the intellect, the *ens commune* or being in general, is not the *ens principium numeri,* nor is it not the being of the time-space continuum; and that the intellect is intellect because it comprehends all things *sub ratione entis.* This comprehension of all things against the horizon of being in general does not mean that man sums up the knowledge of particular objects retrospectively in a universal backward glance, but means that man is intellect (spirit) because, *a priori,* by his self-movement towards being in general he grasps particular objects as parts making up this infinite movement of his. He sees them *a priori* against that horizon of being in general through which man is perpetually receptive to the absolute being of God. Hence St. Thomas can say truly: *Omnia cognoscentia* (meaning, obviously, the spiritually cognitive beings) *cognoscunt implicite Deum in quolibet cognito.*[8] The *concept* of God is, for St. Thomas, the ultimate in all knowledge, but the illuminative pre-concept of being in general, and hence of the absolute self-luminosity of being in the thing which is of absolute "having being," is the prior condition even of the initial conceptual cognition. Thus in each particular cognition God is

[8] *De Ver.* 22, 1, ad 1. See also J. B. Metz, *Christliche Anthropozentrik,* pp. 73-80.

already implicitly known. With this modest indication of the Thomist formulation of the development of our thought we must be content.

Have we not wandered too far from the topic which ought to be engaging our attention? Not at all: we are now right at the heart of a philosophy of religion which, as metaphysical anthropology, is trying to establish the possibility of a revelation to man.

We started off with the question about the implications of the first aspect of our first metaphysical question concerning being for the nature of man as a possible subject of a revelation. We now have found the answer to this in the fact that man "is" absolute receptivity for being pure and simple, in perpetual, unfulfilled ontological differential. Man is the first among those finite cognizands who are fundamentally receptive to the absolute self-luminosity of being. They are receptive in such a way that this receptivity is the condition for the possibility of each particular cognition. There could, therefore, be no sphere of being lying completely beyond this horizon, in which man knows objects (and in this knowledge subsisting in himself), and can take up a relationship to himself and determine his destiny. This basic constitution of man which he affirms implicitly in each of his cognitions and actions we designate as his spirituality. Man is spirit, that is, he lives his life in a perpetual reaching out towards the Absolute, in openness to God. This openness to God is not a contingency which can emerge here or there at will in man, but is the condition for the possibility of that which man is and has to be, even in the most forlorn and mundane life. The only thing which makes him a man is that he is forever on the road to God whether he is clearly aware of the fact or not, whether he wants to be or not, for he is always the infinite openness to the finite for God.[9]

A revelation from God is thus possible only if the subject to whom it is supposed to be addressed *in himself* presents an *a*

---

[9] God does not for his part initiate the relationship; he is already implicit in the openness of this relationship, he can only "suppress" it or "accept" it. See J. B. Metz, "rel. Akt," in *LThK* I, pp. 256-259.

priori horizon against which such a possible revelation[10] can begin to present itself in the first place. Only if this horizon is utterly unlimited is a possible revelation not subject antecedently to law and restriction in respect of what it will be possible to reveal. A revelation which is supposed to disclose the depths of divinity, and which at bottom is the reflex objectification of man's calling to participate in nothing less than the supernatural life of God himself, can only be conceived as possible if man is conceived as spirit. This is to say, man must be the locale of transcendence correlative to being pure and simple. He must necessarily actualize this already perfected transcendence. Every narrower horizon of human knowledge would at once and *a priori* allow possible subjects of revelation to fall outside this horizon and thereby exclude the possibility of their becoming verbally revealed. And so the proposition about the necessarily explicit transcendence of knowledge correlative to being in general as the basic constitution of man as spirit, is the *first* proposition[11] of a metaphysical anthropology, an anthropology that is slanted towards a philosophy of religion as foundation for the possibility of a verbal revelation. The methodical, reflective making explicit in an act of knowledge of this transcendence (which does not merely affirm or prove it as *another* property of man, but as the condition for the possibility of his *mundane* knowledge and action), is the first part of an ontology of the *potentia oboedientialis* for a possible revelation. Thus it belongs right in the very heart of a Christian philosophy of religion.

[10] Here it is of course thrown into relief against a plural, objective, and propositional revelation of individual realities (in their more or less categorical differentiation), and the question of the possibility of such a revelation is posed. Such a question remains perfectly legitimate. But it would also be possible, and ultimately necessary for an adequate philosophy and theology of revelation, to consider the question of gracious, revelatory self-revelation of God to the transcendence of man, through which "transcendental revelation," primarily, a particular object *within* the transcendental horizon does not come newly into being, but leads to the modification of this transcendence *as such*, to its "elevation," clarification, and thereby becomes the place of original revelation, which is of necessity reflected in that categorical revelation in an *historical* process. See J. B. Metz, *Christliche Anthropozentrik*, pp. 97ff.

[11] The second and third propositions are found on pp. 108 and 161 respectively.

Being is luminous, is *Logos,* and can thus be revealed in the Word; this was what we learned in Chapter 3. But man is spirit (a characterization which stamps his whole being as man) and thus has an ear that is open [12] to any word whatsoever that may proceed from the mouth of the Eternal. This is the proposition which takes in the primordial essence of man, the meaning and truth of which we have tried to understand in this chapter.[13]

[12] For a real, delimiting understanding of this sentence, see above, chapter 1, note 8.

[13] Since the proposition offered here of the transcendence in-itself-permanent and the transcending in-itself-permanence of the human spirit takes its bearings from the corresponding thomistic attempt, it is exclusively consummated as transcendental reflexion upon the possibility of the experience of an objective world of things. The attempt to derive this proof from the analysis of the original experience of a *personal co-world* and the question of the inner relationship of both kinds of proof remain outside the scope of our discussion. See below, chapter 11, notes 2 and 6.

PART THREE

THE HIDDENNESS OF BEING

6. THE PROBLEM,
and Preparing the Way for a Solution

These reflections may have given us the beginnings of an insight into the possibility of revelation, but they have also brought us up against a difficulty which seems to contradict the possibility of such revelation. If man is the infinitude of absolute spiritual openness to being in general, and if he must be this because in transcendent openness towards being in general he is spirit first and foremost; if he thus refrains from limiting, *a priori,* the possibilities and breadth of revelation by the limitation of his capacity to receive (that is to say, does not antecedently deny revelation the space within which to unfold itself), then this first proposition of our anthropology arising from the philosophy of religion is the very thing which would seem to make revelation to man impossible once again, in virtue of this basic spiritual constitution of man. If man is the infinitude of absolute intellectual openness to being, if, in scholastic terminology, he is *quodammodo omnia,* then all being appears as knowability, and to fall within the sphere of power of his transcendental openness. Then the opening up of a divine sphere, to which he possesses no key within himself, is *a priori* ruled out, quite apart from the fact that theology knows yet another *new subjective* openness through the *interior* light of grace and faith, which likewise would seem already to have been outstripped by the absolute breadth of man's natural transcendence.[1] Then the presentation by rev-

---

[1] As already mentioned above, this question cannot be entered upon explicitly, because in its reflective foundation it belongs rather to the domain of theology (or to a philosophy of religion theologically oriented). Nevertheless here also we must admit that there is room for an inner illumination of the horizon of human cognition itself through grace

elation of a specific object, because already falling *a priori* within the sphere of human transcendence, could have at most the significance of a contingent and merely temporary aid. In scholastic terminology, it would be possible only through the help of God, and this help would itself be indebted to nature, that is, indebted to the humanly definable constitution of man's essence. Revelation would be an act of the God of the philosophers but not of the God of Abraham, of Isaac, and of Jacob. All of the content of revelation would fundamentally at least then have to be interchangeable with knowledge derivable from the *a priori* structure of man or at least dependent on this structure. Revelation would be merely the first step of philosophy, merely the awareness of the absolute Spirit which breaks in upon man at the level of imagination. It would have to be an awareness that transforms itself of necessity into absolute consciousness, in which the finite spirit becomes aware of its unity with the infinite Spirit in the form of the concept.

Looking at the matter more closely, we see that the same difficulty could have arisen earlier from our first proposition of ontology, and not just from the first proposition of a metaphysical anthropology. Stated in general terms the difficulty we have in mind consists in the fact that our considerations so far would make it seem that there can be no such thing as a revelation in the sense of a free disclosure of something essentially hidden. This is because everything is fundamentally manifest, hence not requiring further revelation. This being the way things are, revelation cannot be anything other than the immanent, necessary unfolding of this manifestation of being, which is *a priori* and for ever given as such in the intellect or spirit. We saw this difficulty first of all with reference to the absolute transcendence of man as intellect. It would seem that for man as intellect, every cognition of being always and in every case can be nothing but the necessary unfolding of his own infinitude. *Too much* would seem to have come from the proposition of

(for a new view by the "light of grace" as a subjective ability, as an "infused virtue"), *if*—and this question is to be posed explicitly here— the openness of human natural transcendence does not after all anticipate all possible objects of revelation *as owed* in the first place.

metaphysical anthropology which we established concerning the place for a possible revelation, that is, the proposition which Vatican I formulated in contradiction of the semi-rationalism of Günther, Hermes, and Frohschammer: *"Hominem ex seipso ad omnis tandem veri et boni possessionem iugi profectu pertingere posse et debere."* [2]

As we have said already, however, this very difficulty seems to arise from the first proposition of our anthropology derived from the philosophy of religion. If being, necessarily and in itself, denotes being-in-oneself, interior illumination and being-reflected-in-oneself; if being is illumined in favor of the thing which is in the measure of its "having being," then it would seem that it must be intrinsically already manifest. This at least to an existent thing which (as *quodammodo omnia*) brings with it an illuminating openness towards all objectivity, that is, towards the spirit. The highest thing which is, would thus have to be already manifest to man, at least to the extent that this man is spirit, and increasingly becomes spirit. Thus revelation would be nothing other than the progressive spiritualization of man himself, according to the interior, natural law of man. God himself would be intrinsically the One who already was uncovered and manifest. Revelation could not be the free act of God, because his light, of necessity, would always radiate and shine within every man. "Light inaccessible" would have to be a contradiction, because *being-light* would by its nature shine upon all things wherever there is space in which it can shine.

And so the question emerges: how can a Christian anthropology and metaphysics expound the nature of man so that, without violating his transcendence relative to being in general or his interior luminosity of being, this transcendence does not anticipate the content of a possible revelation? This free self-disclosure of the personal God must remain possible with God having someone to whom he can utter his free Word of revelation, with what he says being perceptible to man who knows what it means for himself personally. [3]

---

[2] See Denzinger, 1808.

[3] To prevent possible misunderstanding, it should be noted here that grace is the self-revelation of God unto man. This self-revelation is the

Because this difficulty arises out of the first proposition of our general ontology about the luminosity of being, it must be our first task, therefore, to resolve this uncertainty at the level

foundation and the final goal of all revelation. But from this results the fact that revelation, without detriment to its free origin, is an interior quality of the concrete historical essence of man. It is interior insofar as grace, as the divinizing self-revelation, can signify man understood as spirit, without thereby being threatened in its supernaturality and divinity, and *must* ultimately signify *itself,* because there is question here of a personal relationship (of self-revelation), in which it is not the case that "something" occurs to man or beyond him in a purely objective manner, but in which he himself is involved at the center of his spiritual existence. A concept of revelation that takes its starting point with man and his spirituality distorts the comprehension of revelation *interiorly* only when it comprehends the essence of man without taking into account his free historical transcendence (subjectivity), that is, when it refuses to acknowledge the inner different between "nature" and "grace," of the essence of man as historical spirit. *This* true "interiority" of divine revelation in the horizon of the historical spirituality of man, this "interiority" which can yet not be produced or derived from man himself, can also be clarified from another side: man as spirit is *in himself* already ever above himself, without being able to dispose over or materially explain this quality of being above himself, which has been revealed to him and which he has accepted in the completed transcendental liminal experience. This "above-himself" must be explained in divine terms if it is not be mythologically over-questioned in human terms. This fundamental exegesis (which belongs to the human essence) of the human spirit in divine terms does not in itself imply some kind of metaphysical exigency of man of a supernatural self-revelation on the part of God; for this exegesis of divine origin could actually happen in another way also—and we shall refer to this later in this text—and this way is a free keeping-to-himself of God vis-à-vis man. This keeping-to-himself would also be a free historical exegesis of the human spirit and its transcendence derived from God, a transcendence man cannot give to himself. Both kinds of exegesis, however, are *a priori* interior to man in his spirituality and not simply added to it later, because man as a spirit exists as that being which stands open in its essence to the divine exegesis. Man must be understood as a creature in the first place, as a creaturely "nature," in such a way that, in his free self-comprehension (which marks him as a spirit), he is inescapably consigned to the unnameable freedom of God, and must take on the finality of his self-comprehension out of, or from, this divine freedom. This essential consignment of the human self-comprehension to the freedom of God, the "given," thereby, of the "essential history with God," is in the final analysis nothing but the anthropologically oriented term for the condition of man that everything created depends on God in a way that remains always contemporary. That is to say, man in his self-comprehension which is the mark of his humanness, remains dependent upon God, and can never integrate God as a disposable element into his of our general ontology. We will also have to ask why being, in spite of, and in, the fact of its very luminosity is the most hidden thing of all. We must once again go through the process of deduction of the luminosity of being in such a way that the transcendental deduction of the hiddenness of being for each thing which is (that is, that which stands in the unfulfilled ontological differential, in the distance and in the inaccessibility of the absolute existential future [4]), becomes the deduction of the intrinsic inaccessibility of the eternal light to us. Accordingly, we will have to proceed with a further look at our first proposition in anthropology.

This present task in fact coincides with the analytic of the *second* aspect of our initial metaphysical question. The second aspect of the question rested on the fact that in the question about being, something must really be *asked*. To the first note of interrogation is added the second: does being itself admit of being questioned?

It might at first seem as though the infinitude of divine being that is affirmed in the concept were in itself an adequate explanation of the fact that God is essentially the Unknown to the finite spirit. And as the finitude of human spirituality displays itself precisely in the problematicality of his question about being, the analytic of the second aspect would already

---

self-comprehension. The experience and affirmation of the inexhaustibility of God and of his freedom belong to the self-affirmation of man as creature. Man therefore accepts the creaturely dependence peculiar to him in that he interprets himself, in his self-comprehension, not as being simply finally disposable (one might say as "pure nature"), but awaits (as a consummation of his creaturely dependence) a historical exegesis on God's part; we must again emphasize the fact that the factual, supernatural self-revelation of God is only *one* possibility, which man cannot expect or derive, and which is in this sense absolutely *not* owed him, although it belongs to his *inner essence*—it has *in fact* been given by God. This is possibly a new point of departure to arrive at a theological understanding of the possible unity of the quality of not being owed, and at the same time, the immanence of divine grace in man.

[4] Inasmuch as we think of the ontological difference, in the case of God as the being of "absolute having-being" not as simply not present, but think of it as being *perfected* in Him, the question remains open, whether and in what way God is present unto himself absolutely as a "secret." See "Ueber den Begriff des Geheimnisses in der katholischen Theologie," in *Schriften zur Theologie* IV, pp. 51-99.

seem to be completed. We would only need to say: even as spirit, man is finite. The problematicality of being and man's need of questioning himself show the finitude of him who asks. In this way, indeed, the absolute transcendence of man as spirit reveals the infinite. Insofar as this infinitude of being is only absorbed in the unlimited breadth of the pre-concept (this pre-concept on the one hand not representing the infinite in itself, but only affirming it concomitantly as the extreme limit of that unlimited movement of the spirit which we have just described as the pre-concept itself, and on the other hand only featuring as the condition for the possibility of the objectively imaginative knowledge of the finite thing which is, because only thus is it actually known by us to be there at all), to the same extent does the infinitude of God seem to be knowable only in the perception of the *finite* thing which is. This infinitude would thus remain unrecognized by man on his own because it is expressly grasped as such only in the transcendental experience of limitation,[5] that is, of a negatory *remotio* of the finite, at the cognition of which the *excessus* (as the pre-concept is known in Thomist language) is know for the first time. If, therefore, the infinitude of God is known only in the negatory experience of limitation of the finitude of the finite, it appears to be sufficiently unknown, unrevealable, and shut up in its specific self, so that a fresh self-disclosure of the infinite makes sense and still has something which may yet be revealed. The problematicality of being seems thus not merely to exclude the place of some sort of an absolute Gnosis, to the extent that this problematicality uncovers the analogy of "having being" and the finitude of the human spirit (to which we referred earlier), but seems also to manifest sufficiently the essential hiddenness of infinite being in respect of its positive content.

This is all perfectly true and may serve as a first, provisional answer to our uncertainty. But it still seems not enough, and this is why: what has been said so far only makes plain that man, subject to the laws which govern his knowledge, cannot reach

[5] See above, chapter 5, note 2.

positive knowledge of the "beyond," of the eternal world, in his own strength, in spite of the fact that the "beyond," present in his transcendental experience of limitation, is the condition of the possibility of his mundane knowledge. But this seems to establish no more than the mere *de facto* hiddenness of infinite being. We still have not excluded a double assumption: (1) that man on his own might, or even can, reach a stage in which (retaining our former terminology) the absolute breadth of the pre-concept as such would in itself become known without its needing to have a finite object as *"materia,"* by which alone it could be known as the "informing" light of this *materia;* and that this transcendentality of the human spirit, operating within itself, could uphold itself permanently without necessary entrance into the concrete, categorical objectivity of historical existence. Granted, in addition, that this is the only and supreme manner in which a finite spirit could become directly aware of the Absolute as such. Granted that God allows himself to be grasped only in the *excessus* of the finite spirit (without the mediation of a finite object, of a finitely presented "image" in which the object is imagined by the intellect). Then, on such an assumption, the possibility of a positive revelation would be excluded. The highest form of knowing the Absolute would thus be accessible to man in his own right. On the one hand, it would not be merely the common negative theology of rational metaphysics, because such negation would have superseded *a priori* the want of a finite image of a finite object that had to be surmounted and denied. On the other hand, it would not be a *visio beatifica* in the Christian theological sense, because this knowledge of the infinitude of God would come about only in direct grasping of the transcendence of the spirit, that is, in a grasping that was not mediated through an object. Such a supreme knowledge of the Absolute (possible for man, and indeed possible only through his own nature) fundamentally transcends any revelation of God by God in words.

This is no arbitrarily invented assumption, no mere exercise in purely theoretical possibilities, but the basic conception of

77

all non-Christian mysticism [6] such as we find metaphorically expressed in Plotinus's understanding of mysticism, and such as has clearly left its mark even upon the Christian mysticism of writers like Gregory of Nyssa and the Pseudo-Areopagite. The philosophical exposition which Baruzi supplied for the mysticism of the dark night of St. John of the Cross moves in the same direction. In general, wherever we find that mystical piety is in opposition, or at least felt to be in opposition, to the prophetic piety of a revealed religion, the presumption which we have indicated is active. A mystical experience (usually dark-night-ecstatic) in which man, by an *ek-stasis,* a standing outside himself, experiences the infinite beyond his own finitude, is regarded as an experience that surpasses and supersedes all revelation given in words, and not as the graciously unlimited horizon of all word-revelation that is not mythologically enclosed in sheer categories. Whoever thinks that he has ecstatically experienced the infinitude of God in this fashion cannot be told anything more by any human word, which must always be the vehicle even of the revelation of God. Were our thesis of the absolute transcendence of the finite spirit thus to end in a purely natural mysticism, any revelation through the autonomous word of God in a knowledge, deep and yet accessible to man, would be superseded *a priori.* It is true that absolute transcendence might not lead to the absolute philosophy of speculative Gnosis (which to some extent is the sober day-mysticism of reason), but it certainly would lead into a philosophical mysticism of

---

[6] "Non-Christian" is here not meant in the historical sense, but in a fundamental sense, that is, not in the sense of a mystique "outside" of the historical palpability of church Christianity, but as a mysticism that is "natural" in a strictly theological sense. A "mysticism" of the realization of the transcendence of man brought about and sanctified through the self-revelation of God in his grace does not exclude the historical word of revelation, because it is already revelation in the original sense, and comes into its own and is thematized in the history of the revelation of the word. Inasmuch as "transcendental revelation" and "categorical revelation" in the sense of the human being as a historical spirit and God as incarnate Logos (both of these being, in turn, interrelated), comprise an inner and ever-whole unity, the categorical self-explication of "transcendental revelation" remains the work of God in the history of salvation and revelation, that is, the objective reality of the one divine revelation itself.

dark-night ecstasy. Both, however, would have the same destructive consequences for the possibility of an autonomous revelation by God. Mystical piety, even if only to the extent of a dark sensing of God in the limitless infinity of the spirit itself, which finds its springs in natural means and regards itself as unsurpassable, would always already have superseded any prophetic piety of the revealed word in its historical confinement.

(2) There is also a second assumption arising from our proposition concerning the absolute transcendence of the spirit which would make revelation impossible, unless our explanation of the hiddenness of God precisely in the transcendence of man has already been sufficient to dispose of such an assumption. We might say: the fact of the absolute openness of the spirit, of its dynamic self-movement in the pre-concept of infinite being, requires the possibility of a direct vision of God as the sole, ultimate fulfillment of the absolute breadth of the spirit. Such a vision might then perhaps require an action on the part of God, but this would be merely the facilitation of the natural self-fulfillment of man. The natural goal of man as spirit would be the *visio beatifica*. The peak of his spiritual life in its immanent, natural development would be not just a dark-night-ecstatic experience of the infinitude of God in the experience of the fluctuating infinitude of his own spirit that surmounted all finitude, but the direct vision of the substance of the infinite being of God, presenting itself in its own self. Thus we would have arrived more or less at the heretical view of Begarden mysticism: *Quod quaelibet intellectualis natura in seipsa naturaliter est beata, quodque anima non indiget lumine gloriae ipsam elevante ad Deum videndum et eo beate fruendum.*[7] For a start, we may not simply say in reply to this assumption that such a question about the indebtedness or graciousness of the *visio beatifica* has nothing to do with the question about the possibility of revelation, for the two questions deal with quite different things. But this is not correct. If the *visio beatifica* (which discloses the essence of God more than any possible revelation in mere words and finite symbols) seems to be the

[7] Denzinger, 475.

natural goal of man, then a revelation as essentially a free act of the God who discloses himself from free grace is no longer conceivable. At most, it could be thought of as an anticipatory making known in words of God, who is in principle and in the last analysis always manifest to the human spirit.

Here there is a basic objection that can significantly be made: the absolute breadth and unlimitation of the transcendence of the human spirit has been affirmed by us as a condition for the possibility of an objective knowledge of the finite thing which "is," and of the subsisting-in-himself of man. By thus making possible this mode of being of a finite existent thing (a mode which turns the thing into a spiritual being), this transcendence has reached its goal, even though its whole breadth is never directly filled up by manifest infinite being. And because we were able to demand and to prove this transcendence only as condition of *this* possibility; because we did not demonstrate it as a function exclusively possessing within itself a determination, neither may we demand that in itself, independently of the whole structure of the human spirit, it should find a fulfillment which would be different from that on account of which this transcendence was demanded. Because in philosophical anthropology we acknowledge only human knowledge, to which belongs (in addition to this one condition of possibility, the pre-concept correlative to being in general) the presentation of a finite object, so that we are simultaneously aware of the presentation itself, therefore, philosophically, we can accomplish nothing with regard to the possibility of the fulfillment of this transcendental breadth of the spirit without the mediation of a finite, sensible object. The right to an inner possibility of a *visio beatifica* would thus remain in doubt.

This is all true and worth bearing in mind, but the knowledge that the *visio beatifica* cannot unequivocally be demonstrated to be the natural end of man is no proof that it is essentially supernatural. It cannot be said that man has no title to it whatever, that, in spite of man's absolute transcendence, God confronts man as the one who is for ever unknown, present in this way as an object of a possible revelation. We might even enquire whether man in himself, that is, by nature, is orientated towards the infinite (supposing that we can prove that he is so orientated) only in order to hover in endless movement, a wanderer through the wide expanse of finitude, able to greet the infinite only from afar, never once finding the road that leads directly to the face of God. St. Thomas himself speaks of a *desiderium naturale* for the immediate vision of God. Whatever the more exact meaning of this statement may be for St. Thomas (many theologians have written on the subject and many views have been expressed), it shows nonetheless that St. Thomas saw that relationships obtained between the spirituality of man (his *natura*), its immanent dynamism (*desiderium*) on the one hand, and the *visio beatifica* on the other—relationships, moreover, which arise not merely from the actual calling of man in grace to have an immediate vision of God, but which precede it and are "natural."

Whatever has just been said of this uncertainty in terms of the presumed possibility of a *visio beatifica* applies *mutatis mutandis* to the uncertainty relative to the assumption of a nature-mysticism. The possibility of such a thing, in the manner described above, allows of no positive proof, at least not in an *a priori* metaphysical anthropology which can proceed only from the essence and function of a transcendence which would have meaning and purpose only if there were, or could be, no such mysticism. On the other hand, however, what has been argued so far does not positively exclude such an assumption either.

And so the question as to why the absolute transcendence of the spirit (as the *a priori* opening up of function for revelation, along with the pure luminosity of pure being), has not automatically superseded revelation even as a possibility has not yet been solved completely.

So far, this is what has been expounded. Man stands before God who is, at least temporarily, the Unknown. He is the infinite who, in his infinitude, can be known by man only in the negation implied in the ultimate limit of all finitude, an implication which is the condition of the objective grasping of a finite thing which is. However, in such a mode of the knowledge of God, he remains veiled within the positive content of his infinitude. This does not yet make clear whether or not his veiledness is more than the *not-yet-knowing* of man himself, that is, man who, as finite spirit, has not yet arrived at the end of his spiritual development. So far we have established the hiddenness of God *in terms of man,* in terms, indeed, of the merely factual structure of his spiritual nature. We have reviewed, in other words, the blindness of man rather than the hiddenness of God in itself. But only if such hiddenness of God in itself stands inviolate and distinct from all finite spirits (not just man in the *de facto* structure of his cognition) can the possibility of a revelation of God be conceived as a free act of God. Not until we go beyond the free knowledge that God is more than what we have hitherto known of him by our human knowledge, as established in anthropology, and discover that he can speak or remain silent, can we conceive of an actual speech of God (if it does occur) as it really is. This is the priceless act of his personal love before which man falls upon his knees in adoration.

7. THE FREE UNKNOWN

Has an absolute transcendence in the face of the sheer luminosity of being not already, by its very nature, surpassed any possible revelation? The preceding chapter has made this uncertainty obvious and established a few provisional insights that are important for the solution of the problem. Because of the finitude of our knowledge in the absolute and infinite breadth of our transcendence, God is the one who is for ever unknown, as far as the factual knowledge of the human spirit is concerned. Moreover, the immediate vision of God cannot be demonstrated to be the natural end of man. This is not, however, an exhaustive answer to our question. Even on these terms it is still conceivable that God *in himself* might be the intrinsically manifest reality. We still have not clearly proved the possibility of a revelation as the free self-disclosure of God. Only revelation of that sort establishes philosophically the basic autonomy and distinctiveness of theology over and against philosophy, and only the knowledge of the content of this discipline elevates the philosophy of religion to become theology.

And so we take up afresh the second aspect of our general question about being—the *problematicality* of being, which lies at the heart of the very possibility of asking the question. To the extent that we may ask questions about being, and to the extent that man is able to, and must, enquire about being as a whole, he already knows of being as a whole, he is already, in anticipation, in touch with it. By this he has already affirmed the inner luminosity of being as such. But why does he affirm this inner luminosity of being at all? Is he perhaps that thing which is, in the act of being, being present-to-itself, merged with its own self-luminosity? If that is the way things are, then

83

either man would have to be the thing which is of absolute "having being" (namely, God himself), or the absolute being of God would have to display itself to him automatically. If man in his own luminosity were the thing which is of absolute "having being," or possessed in himself this luminosity as the immediate cause of his own self-fulfillment (in that which we call the *visio beatifica*), then the being under discussion, which is affirmed to be luminous in itself, could not be at the same time basically unintelligible to man. For the universal luminosity of being (given only in the transcendental experience of *limitation*) is not identical with immediate luminosity *in* itself, as is proper to the thing which is of absolute "having-being" in perfect ontological identity (and differential). Nor is it to be conceived in a *visio beatifica*,[1] should such a thing be possible at all.

An answer through this sort of "having-being" would have gone so far beyond the question as to make the question itself impossible. These considerations fundamentally and completely rule out the possibility of an ontology and thus a philosophy of religion, upon the ground of ontologism and its disguised twin-brother, rationalism.

Whence, then, arises the necessity of affirming the luminosity of being at all? It is not obvious with regard to the absolute being of God, nor does the essential connection of these two concepts appear from their sheer conceptual contents (being and knowability) alone. The reason for this necessity was already indicated in our deduction of the first proposition of general ontology. The fact that real questions about being can be asked

---

[1] This is not the place to give an exact ontological explication of the theological concept of the *visio beatifica* in relation to the ontology here posited. Without such an explanation it remains clear that the *visio beatifica* cannot be coexistent with that liminal experience in which we know of the being on the whole in removed and rejecting (and in this sense incomplete) difference. When we declare here that both divinity and the *visio beatifica* are incompatible with the transcendental liminal experience which produces the luminosity of being on the whole solely in the *modus* of interrogation, we do not claim thereby that the *visio beatifica* means the *same* indisputability of "having-being," that is, calls to appearance the *same* perfection of the ontological difference as in the case of God himself. See the article on "Geheimnis" cited above, chapter 6, note 4.

must be explicitly affirmed, because it has already been affirmed implicitly in the question that occurs of necessity in the existence of man. The man who is able to refrain from enquiring about being need not affirm the proposition that being is knowable. In every judgment and action of man, however, there is a knowing of being. Whenever man has anything at all to do, in thought or action, with any separate thing which is, the question is put about the nature of being, of which he already has an anticipatory knowledge in those very thoughts and actions. The evidence of metaphysics, therefore, is founded upon the necessity which is manifest in human existence. The ultimate metaphysical evidence available to man is not material evidence in the sense of an insight into being in general, an insight, that is, into the absolute being of God, but formal evidence based upon man's need to be what he is, namely, one who in all his thought and action is an enquirer into being, and who, in spite of questioning and the unknowability of being for man, always affirms the right to question and luminosity of being. These he can affirm only to the extent that he affirms his existence, and because he has to affirm his existence in its human uniqueness. The opening up to man of being in general occurs essentially, in the last analysis, in man's unavoidable taking possession of his own existence.

The existence of man which is thus drawn into the innermost center of the examination of an ultimate necessity is a sheerly factual thing—a *contingency*. To dispute this fact would be to dispute its finitude. This is shown by the fact that in his transcendental experience of limitation man presents being to himself, intrinsically and as far as he himself is concerned, as something that does not lie at his disposal. To dispute this fact would be to attempt to push man into the center of the infinitude of being that opens up within human transcendence, thus annulling its unknowability for man. Man must, therefore, accept his existence in its contingency, if his existence is to be human existence, that is, if he is to stand before the luminosity of being which must necessarily be affirmed. The first metaphysical affirmation of an absolute necessity is, at one and the same time, the affirmation of human accidentality and "abandonment." Only he who is set on his own finitude is aware of the true infinitude of being.

What do we conclude from all of this? We have here a starting point for a new, fundamental insight both into our general ontology (which always includes a statement about God), and also into our metaphysical anthropology. Now we must develop this fresh insight with reference to *general ontology*.

Let us begin with the characteristic structure of human existence, which has manifested itself in all of our considerations so far. Man in his subsistence within himself and in the objectivity of his cognition and action experiences a necessary relationship to himself. Of necessity he must be present to himself, must affirm himself, must posit himself. In virtue of this necessity he enquires into being in general, and to the extent that, in the necessity of this acceptance of his being, he enquires, he knows being in general. He affirms the luminosity of being and his own transcendence with reference to being in general, and so he stands before God. Insofar as he must *enquire,* he affirms his contingency necessarily. And in necessarily affirming this he affirms his existence in and despite his contingency as unconditional, as absolute. In other words: because the affirmation of the *contingent* fact is inescapably *necessary,* an absoluteness is disclosed in the contingence itself, the inescapability with which the contingent fact intrinsically requires its affirmation. In spite of its accidentality its existence intrinsically excludes the possibility of its denial. That is to say, however, that man possesses the necessary relationship of an absolute position in his finite, contingent existence. Solely in this necessity of a cognitive relationship to the non-necessary is the transcendence with respect to intrinsically luminous being in general affirmed.

In the absolute delimitation of an accidental as absolute we experience *will.* Such a delimitation must inwardly be more than merely static insight. It must be will, for pure comprehension as such can find the basis of this delimitation only in the object itself. An accident as such, however, provides no reason within its own "thisness" to affirm it absolutely. Were its mere *occurrence* itself to be regarded as the reason of the absolute delimitation of its "thisness," then this existence would be posited as necessary. For only such an existence can be the reason for an out and out affirmation. This existence would thus be the necessary existence of an accident, which is a contradiction. Thus the delimitation of the accident does not find the reason for itself unequivocally from the thing delimited as such. The reason is hence first of all the reason for the delimitation, and only then of the thing delimited as such. Will, however, is such a reason. The necessary absolute delimitation which posits existence in contrast to its accidentality is therefore will. At the foundation of existence, that is, at the heart of the primary transcendence with reference to being, there takes place the (necessary) act of the will. The opening up of being for existence is effected through will as an *inner* factor of knowledge itself. First of all, we have to trace this knowledge more closely in the direction in which it includes a statement about being itself, that is, in the direction of general ontology. The results which emerge for metaphysical anthropology will not be examined until the next chapter.

Man's will with regard to himself appears as the inner condition of the possibility and necessity of the question about being, and thus as the condition of knowing about being in general. What is the effect of this on the nature of being and its relationship to the finite thing which is, and to finite human existence in particular? At the foundation of human existence there constantly takes place a necessary and absolute affirmation of the accidental reality that is man himself, that is, of will. At the same time, however, the luminosity of being in general is affirmed. That is to say, this necessary intentional affirmation makes that which is affirmed in this way (because found as strange and presented to us) appear in its contingency as foreign in intention, and capable of conception only as the consequence of a *free* absolute delimitation of the non-necessary. For this absolute delimitation of accidental human existence would not emerge originally from a *free* will were the basic luminosity of being as such to be nullified. A *necessity* in the delimiting of an accidental, known *as* accidental and hence as something not conceived as to be necessarily delimited, could emerge only from an obscure cause, not from a cause that is self-luminous, not from a cause that is conscious of itself. If the delimited accidental reality that is man were to arise from a cause, the delimiting of which arises therefrom with absolute necessity, then either that which is delimited would be as necessary as the delimiting itself, or the reason for the delimiting would be of such a kind that its illumination through a *logical* link between it (the delimiting, and the thing delimited, with reference to accidentality and necessity) would be excluded by the specific nature of the reason. Both assumptions, however, are untenable, the first because the thing delimited is accidental, the second because being, in other words the reason for the delimiting, must ultimately be luminous. But an illumination of the connection between a necessary delimiting and an accidental, non-necessary thing delimited cannot be conceived. From this it follows that the deliberate *necessary* delimiting of an accidental, such as occurs in the affirming attitude of human existence towards itself, can be conceived only when it is itself affirmed as delimited by a *free* deliberate act of delimitation. Human delimiting is necessary because it is a thing delimited by a free volition. The necessary absolute delimitation of an accidental, which as such affirms the luminosity of being, can thus be but the delimited resultant and extension (necessary because posited) of a free deliberate absolute delimitation of this accidental. This free deliberate primeval delimitation of the thing which is, that is, man (for in all our studies we are concerned all the time with the delimiting of this very thing), can, however, be nothing but the delimiting of absolute being, of God. We have already pointed out that in general God must be affirmed as the reason for or cause of all that is. At present we are concerned only with pointing out further that this founding of the finite thing which is by God is a free and deliberate act.

Man, then, in his necessary absolute attitude to his contingency (an attitude which affirms the luminosity of his being), affirms himself as the free deliberate delimiting of God. He knows himself to be supported by the *free* power of God. This implies that in the last analysis he does not face the absolute being of God (the ultimate horizon of his cognitive advance, as an immovable ideal which, *semper quiescens,* must always stand open to his assault), but as a free autonomous power. God is the objective of reaching out of the human spirit, but he is that precisely because he appears as the free power which stands in contradistinction from the finite. Thus when finite intellect knows him, such knowledge is based upon his own free delimiting of the finite, upon what we call the creation. In this way it is already always an answer to a free world that the Absolute has spoken. This is implicitly affirmed as just such a free act, if the finite spirit in virtue of his transcendence feels himself to be founded upon reference to the Absolute.

Let us sum up all the essentials. As a spirit, and as such a knowing absolute being, man stands distinct from this absolute being who is a free autonomous powerful *person*. This personal countenance of God is not an attribute resulting from the retrospective fitting out of absolute being with human features. The personality of God is displayed in the self-disclosure of absolute being before human transcendence, for this appears through man in the question mark associated with all being, which at the same time is problematicality.

The cognitive encounter with a free person who thus subsists in himself alone is such as to allow the known to remain unknown. On account of freedom a person is disclosed ultimately only through the deliberate act of the person himself who is to be known. There is indeed no preparatory *a priori* distinct from the free delimitation of a non-necessary thing, in terms of which the latter may be known. It can be known only in terms of *itself*. Insofar as the free delimitation of God determines his personal relationship to us, the knowledge of this relationship is always dependent upon his own free purpose.

Thus man stands already constantly and fundamentally before a God of revelation [2]—a God, moreover, who acts in history. If

[2] "Revelation" is here understood in a bivalent, yet for our purposes decisive sense: inasmuch as man in his transcendental necessity experiences himself as standing before the *free* Godhead, his transcendental self-comprehension is always enveloped in the infinity of this divine freedom and in the pro-visionality of the setting-free already experienced; for the freed *as such* is always understood in that the genuine other possibility in each case, either passed over or denied in the setting-free, remains present as the condition to the experience of freedom or being-

God the transcendent faces man as free power from the very start, awareness of only two conditions is required for him to be recognized as the God of a revelation that might possibly proceed from God in another way than that which has occurred in any case in the free delimitation of man. The possibility of a limitation of his freedom must still be not quite at an end through the creation of this finite thing which knows him. In other words, the possibilities of a limitation must not be exhausted by this delimitation already accomplished. His creation so far may not be the exhausting of his free possibilities. God must still possess free scope for his free action towards his creature, for this is the condition of any free delimitation at all, and of its recognition by the one who is limited.[3] On the other side, too, the creature must still have room for the material knowledge of such a fresh act of God towards it. In a word, there must still be an object of a further free act as the object of a cognition that is not yet at an end. Both of these conditions have been fulfilled. The free delimitation of the finite and accidental by God already includes the fact that the further action of God upon this limited creature cannot be simply and in every respect the logically calculable consequence of this first delimitation. For the contingency of this delimited finite condition already implies changeability and thus always faces the possibility of a fresh free will of God. It is never the unambiguous prejudgment of the direction of the free action of God. The second condition likewise has been fulfilled. The horizon of possible objects opened up in the transcendence of the spirit is in principle wider

set-free, in its deprivation. In this however, inversely, every factual expression of the divine freedom always appears also as the "revelation" of its other possibility—if only in the *moduus* of deprivation and material indefineability, that is, *every* free relationship of God to man becomes "revelation."

[3] Man can recognize himself as the freed creature of God, and assume himself to be such, only in that he knows himself, in his transcendence (as which he exists), to be inevitably exposed to that freedom, that the freedom of God announced in creation remains the ever inevitable destiny of his affirmed creaturehood. In other words: the inevitable exposing of man to the freedom of God and its un-derivable possibilities belong to his self-comprehension *as a creature*. See also chapter 6, note 2 and *passim*.

than all that is not the direct vision of the absolute being of God. As long, therefore, as this is not determined, and as long as it cannot be represented as the end of absolute transcendence of the spirit already immanently required, there is always basically still room left for the acceptance of the disclosure of God who in his freedom determines himself in such or such a manner.

To the extent that man in his absolute, not yet finally fulfilled, transcendence stands before the free God, he stands, in his primary ontological questioning, as the excellence of his essential constitution. He stands before the possibility of the free action of God upon him, thus before the God of a possible material revelation. To the extent that every free act is always original, a once-for-all thing incalculable in terms of all that is "external," such a revelation is not simply the continuance of a disclosure of being which has already been begun, even if this disclosure has been begun tentatively and along an unambiguous direction in man with his natural knowledge of God. It is not simply a continuance even if this natural knowledge of God is correctly understood and perfected only where it constantly knows itself to be referred back to the sovereign freedom of God and immersed within that freedom.

If we would properly assess the import of our discussion so far we must note the following. It is not meant to prove that there are mysteries in the depths of the Godhead which on the one hand are part of the necessary essence of God (for example, the Trinity), and on the other are essentially mystery, that is, accessible only through the free self-disclosure of God in grace. Our purpose has been more modest but no less significant. It was to demonstrate that man *through his transcendence* and in the specifically human mode of this transcendence is not simply placed before the absolute being of God as *semper quiescens,* but before that God who may possibly still undertake free action towards man, and for knowledge of whom there is still room left in man's cognition. Whether this God will act towards man and if so, in what way; whether he will be able through this action to reveal mysteries of his own necessary essence, remains to be seen and may be left to the *a posteriori* knowledge arising from the actual revelation of this God.

91

It is of decisive importance to our study, however, to see that man's transcendence towards the intrinsically luminous being that is completely knowable is at the same time at least openness before a God who deals freely with man. This action of God cannot be calculated from the human side, so that transcendence towards the absolute being of God is a standing before the *mysterium inperscrutabile* whose ways are unfathomable and whose decrees incalculable. If this is the way things are, then knowledge of God as absolute being is simultaneously a having to reckon with a possible action of God that goes beyond the act that has already taken place in the free delimitation of the finite spirit. This is sufficient, however, for our task, for man has always been essentially the listener for a possible revelation from God. That is to say, if this moment of standing before God coincides with his moment of standing before a possible revelation of God, then some sort of revelation does in fact take place. God speaks or is silent. What man always and essentially hears is the speaking or the silence of a free God who subsists in himself alone. Otherwise, he would not be spirit. Being spirit is not itself a claim upon God's utterance, but if God does not speak, man's spirit hears God's very silence. Otherwise, he would not be spirit, because if he were not, he would not be standing before the living free God as a spirit. As spirit, man stands before the living Free Spirit, the Spirit who discloses himself or who remains silent. For this reason, in virtue of his creaturely ontological constitution, man can never be indifferent towards a revelation that may possibly proceed from the living God.

As already indicated and if we understood our statement correctly, we may say that, in virtue of his nature as spirit, man constantly and essentially hears a revelation from God. In a metaphysical sense revelation is simply the free action of God, which is thus always and of necessity a disclosure of his essence that goes further than the disclosure positively and materially granted through the constitution of finite spirit and of all that this embraces. Whoever stands as one free person before another forthwith discloses himself. He discloses himself precisely as the one who he desires to be in the eyes of the other, either the hidden or the revealed.[4] In this sense, revelation occurs of necessity. Precisely because revelation in this sense necessarily occurs (not just *might occur*), man must necessarily reckon with revelation in the usual theological sense. He must reckon with a possible speech from God that breaks his silence and discloses his depths to the finite spirit. This is so for the very reason that revelation, in the metaphysical sense given, is necessary, and because it is man who is always addressed by it. Revelation is not the free decision of God in disclosing himself *or* in withholding himself, but the actual disclosure of his hidden essence. Obviously, we cannot say of this revelation that it comes necessarily to man in virtue of his nature. On the contrary, it is essentially free.

[4] To "stand before another as a free person" of course always implies a certain openness to begin with, but just the kind a person has who can refuse himself.

8. THE FREE LISTENER

We are trying to carry out a metaphysical analytic of the nature
of man with a view to producing a philosophy of religion that is
aware of itself as an ontological explanation of man as subject
of a possible revelation. Because metaphysical anthropology is
always at the same time general ontology (being able to exist at
all only within such a metaphysic), our analytic of human
existence is always a statement about being in general and about
the absolute being of God in particular. Thus it is clear that such
statements of general ontology always have significance for the
philosophy of religion as well. In the last chapter the transcendental analytic of our general enquiry into being, that is, into
the possibility of man's asking the questions, was carried out
with a view to discovering what insight this would yield for
general ontology. We discovered that the absolute being of God,
seen as the ultimate objective of human transcendence, supports
in existence the finite existent thing without at the same time
bringing to an end the possibility of self-revelation to the
creature. Thus in spite of its openness to the transcendence of
the finite spirit, the absolute being of God appears as a being
that speaks or remains silent, in other words as the God of a
possible revelation through his word, because he is the God of
a necessary revelation through speech *or* silence. And so the
basic human situation is always essentially one of standing before
a God, free with the as yet unfulfilled and incalculable possibilities of his freedom; and this is therefore a standing before him
who acts in history, before the God of revelation. In this way
we arrived at the second proposition of our general doctrine of
being (a statement about the absolute being of God): the absolute being of God is free being vis-à-vis the finite created thing.

94

Now we must answer the question: what insight into the nature of *man* emerges from the analytic of our general enquiry into being under this second aspect? In the last chapter we already dealt somewhat with this subject in our study of the general doctrine of being. What is that existent being who, in virtue of his essential constitution as finite spirit, necessarily enquires about being. He stands before the free God and affirms God's freedom through the characteristic nature of his question about being. Therefore, he must reckon with a divine freedom through which God is able to disclose himself in such a way as to reveal his nature, a revelation that is not deducible *a priori* from some other source. The conclusions of the last chapter were equally insights belonging to an analytic of the nature of man. In this context it has also been demonstrated that at the foundation of finite knowledge of being there occurs a deliberate and necessary affirmation of one's own contingent existence. Being is revealed to the human spirit through and in a reflexive attitude to oneself—though not in the sense that the knowledge of being is preceded by a blind urge that makes itself known first in dull incomprehension and then gives rise to cognition (that is, spirit), which had remained imprisoned in this inert substratum, unable to shine through it at all. That would be a superficial and totally false version of the important insight which we mentioned as the prerequisite of the insights we have already gained. The insight we speak of has nothing in common with a metaphysical irrationalism, other than the grain of truth that must lie hidden even in such a false view. If will is affirmed as a factor that is contained in the knowledge itself, this is only to affirm a thesis that is obvious in Thomistic ontology. Being is always spirit and will, *verum* and *bonum*. Cognition, because it is being, and because being is intelligible, cannot be adequately comprehended in its *own* nature, except it also be comprehended as will. That will is not *merely* the inner factor of knowledge, but also a transcendental determination of being which in a certain sense goes beyond cognition, is another question that does not concern us any further at the moment. However, beginnings of this insight were already indicated in the last chapter.

Because this insight into the intentional or deliberative factor in knowledge is the point of departure for our further studies, and because for other reasons it is important to be perfectly clear on this point, we must take up this question once again.

The necessary affirmation by man of the luminosity of being as such is based upon the necessity of the affirmative attitude to himself. This is found in man through the necessity of his being able to observe himself both in cognition and action. In such a necessary act of relationship with himself, however, man affirms himself as finite, as accidental. To the extent that he necessarily affirms himself, his existence is something unavoidable in spite of his accidentality. This is something to be accepted utterly, something in this sense absolute. In spite of its accidentality, because this affirmation is *pure,* undelimited definition of the finite knowing subject, it is not a form of questioning, or of his choosing between yes and no. Man's existence demands an absolute affirmation. It has to be affirmed, and, in spite of its contingency, it has always demanded this outlook. In this irrefutable acceptance of accidentality there is acceptance of a dual possibility that is already determined in one direction. It implies in itself a free choice. In itself it does not determine or indicate the resultant choice in any one direction. But it does cause the spirit to affirm the luminosity of being in general through the transcendence that emerges in the process. How is this possible? Luminosity denotes fundamental comprehensibility. The accidental seems, however, to be fundamentally incomprehensible. A thing is comprehended only if it can be traced back to its cause, only if it can be seen against the background of the reason for existence, and as it were, seen as arising as a necessary consequence of this or that reason or cause. Our proposition about the comprehensibility of being in itself did indeed arise from the fact that in the first question about being every possible object of cognition is already anticipated under the general aspect of being in general. There can, therefore, be no existent thing that does not automatically and objectively fit into the context of being in general. For this very reason every thing is comprehensible. A contingent thing that in its sheer contingency existed unattached and in absolute baseless isolation, would not be able to fit into the notion of being by reason of the nature of its own being. This integration into being in general is the cause of the comprehensibility of the particular existent thing. Anything so utterly indetermined would be fundamentally incomprehensible. Moreover, such a state of affairs would contradict our first general proposition of ontology. The only thing that is comprehensible is *either* the absolute being of God himself because, as the ultimate object of the human pre-concept, it gives rise to the openness of the spirit to the totality of its possible objects of knowledge, *or* the particular finite existent thing which is the object of cognition insofar as this latter is grasped as based upon the absolute being of God. Were things otherwise, this particular existent thing would have no reason for being comprehensible, for such comprehensibility implies integration within the absolute horizon of possible objects of cognition. If this integration is posited, either it must itself form the absolute horizon of cognition (which it cannot because it is finite), or it must be grasped as intrinsically joined with this horizon of cognition, that is, it must have its cause or reason (that of its being and comprehensibility, of its integration in the horizon of being in general) in the absolute being of God. That this delimitation, this basing of the finite existent thing upon the absolute being of God, must be conceived as something intentional and free has already been sufficiently expounded in the previous chapter.

This is the point where we must resume our previous discussion at an even deeper level. We must ask the question: does all this reconcile the contingency of human existence (which must necessarily be affirmed by man) with the luminosity of being in general? At first, it would seem that the incomprehensabilities of the thing, or the inability of seeing where any particular contingent existent thing fits within rationalizing unity in being, is merely being transposed from the contingency of the thing itself to the contingency of the delimitation, in other words from the contingency of the thing to the contingency of the freedom of God.

To begin with, we have to concede that that which is delimited, in its contingency, remains obscure *to us,* in spite of its delimitation and comprehensibility. For the delimitation appears to us only in the thing delimited, and so possesses for us, to whom the delimitation of freedom is not *of itself* disclosed, the same obscurity as the delimited thing itself. But the contingency of the finite thing is to be reconciled not with *our* finite knowledge of being, but with that luminosity which is appropriate to being. And we must ask further: is the contingent, in its free delimitation, luminous even in God himself? Is not free delimitation (as opposed to the thing delimited) once more something incomprehensible? For that which is free has no cause from which it is seen to derive necessarily, and from which it is thus made luminous. In other words, does God, who is free, himself comprehend his free action? Or does this action, in its "non-contingency," its "causelessness," confront him as something incomprehensible?

It is perfectly obvious that this problem cannot and need not be solved in such a way as to demand that the required luminosity of the free act possess a comprehensibility that is *a priori* made to fit the answer to this question *in advance*. We are as yet engaged in the initial exposition of the problem of being in general. We are concerned primarily with acquiring the correct concept of the luminosity of being, and this concept should, in fact, turn out to be the nature of that being about which we enquire. It is from the freedom of the action of knowing itself that we shall acquire the correct concept of luminosity. Thus we are perfectly justified in putting the question the other way around: how are we to grasp the luminosity of being so as to be able to grasp the free action of God as being in itself luminous?

Fundamentally, knowledge is the self-luminosity of the thing which "possesses" being. Thus, where the thing which is is perfectly present to itself, there is perfect cognition. Where taking possession of oneself has reached its limit, there too is the nature of knowledge fulfilled. In its original nature, however, the free act is not so much the delimitation of something different or alien to itself, but is the fulfillment of its *own na*ture. A free act is a taking possession by a thing of itself, that is, of the reality of its own creative power over itself. Thus it is a *coming to oneself,* a *being present to oneself,* within oneself. The act is free, underived delimitation. It is not something standing apart, as different and contingent, as distinct from the one who in the act of knowledge knows it *in the delimitation itself*. For this reason the act is *illuminated* for him himself, even though it may be obscure to *another* who can only be aware of that which is delimited and not the actual delimitation of the act. It is precisely the fact that the free act belongs to the innermost meaning of being subsisting within itself, which demonstrates at once that it is luminous in all its depth to the free self but obscure to any other being which is differentiated from that self. The free act is that which most of all exists in the being where it originates. Hence it is that which in itself and for itself is luminosity par excellence. At the same time, it is an act which is least of all assimilable to another. It is luminous in itself, obscure in another. It can be luminous and comprehensible in another only if that other cooperates in the free act, if he himself loves it. And so the free act is illumined in itself. Should it appear to be obscure and incomprehensible, it is so only to an intelligent being that desires to comprehend it while remaining outside it. This is not to contradict its comprehensibility of the act, but to demand that the cognition enter into sympathy, as it were, with the free act so that in this way it can comprehend it and the thing which it limits. This occurs when the comprehending does not try to grasp the free act of the other as already delimited, but enters into the delimitation itself, allowing it to arise as a consequence of its own being as well. In this process that which is free can be present to itself and thus can be grasped.

In passing let us note: the concept of luminosity which we introduced even before our last investigation, and which we defined in terms of freedom, demonstrates the possibility of reconciling freedom and comprehensibility. We defined comprehensibility in advance as the possibility of integration within the rationalizing context of being. This possibility can be made rational either by that which comprehends the being of the absolute being of God himself (the ultimate objection of all human desire to comprehend), or through the ontological linking of the finite existent thing with this absolute being of God. This definition applied to a free act of God shows at once that a free act is comprehensible—moreover, that it is intrinsically comprehensible. But we avoided this shorter road, preferring the reverse process from freedom to luminosity, because in this way new and important insights arose.

And so—resuming our reflections—the finite has its foundation or reason in the free luminous act of God. This free act which is present to itself is *love*. For love is the self-luminous act of movement towards a person in his underived uniqueness. It is this very inclination which God manifests in the delimitation of a finite existent thing. In such action he desires to enter into his own free creative act as into the "power" of the gift of being, and in this he selflessly endows the other with his own "having being." The finite contingent thing is illumined in the free love of God for himself and therein for his freely delimited work. In this, love appears as the lamp of the knowledge of the finite and, because we know the infinite only through the finite, as the light of our knowledge in general. In its ultimate essence knowledge is but the bright radiance of love. Any act of knowledge of a finite being which does not want to see itself, in the last analysis, as something which reaches the perfection of its own essence in love, turns into darkness. Such a being is compelled either falsely to present the contingent as a necessary thing, or to let it remain in a state of absolute incomprehensibility, that is, of non-being which is constantly contradicted by knowledge—or to explain the thing which is, in terms of blind urge, in the depths of which no light shines.

Insofar, therefore, as God in his love for himself loves freely as the delimiting power of the finite, he lovingly comprehends the finite itself. In this love, that which is delimited is elevated into the light of being. To the extent that God loves the finite it participates in the luminosity of being, and this is the only way such participation is possible. Only in the logic of love does knowledge arrive at the comprehension of the freedom of being.

It is not our intention merely to illumine obscurities in our earlier considerations. To enquire into the being of man in this way is to illuminate the second aspect of our question about being. What is more, we are already on the way to achieving this illumination. If now it has become clearer to us why the absolute delimitation of the contingent being illumines itself in this transformation of mere cognition into cognitive love; if we now see that the affirmation of a contingent thing by God in cognitive love does not militate against the luminosity of being in general, then also we achieve an insight into the *consequence* of this affirmation by man. It is a consequence of the power of God's free love, which in itself is luminous and creative and is fundamentally a love for himself, that engenders being.

In other words, at the heart of the transcendence of the finite spirit there arises a love of God. Man's openness to the absolute being of God is the affirmation of his own existence, and vice versa. This constitutes a deliberate attitude to himself and, at the very foundation of his nature, a reaching out of finite love towards God. This is because the desire of the spirit in its affirmation of the contingent must rest upon God's affirmation of his own nature. This means that man's approach to God, achieved through knowledge constituting man's nature as spirit, possesses within itself a love of God as the deepest factor of this very knowledge. The love of God is not something which can be merely added retrospectively to this knowledge, but, as the deepest factor of knowledge, is both its *condition* and its *cause*.

In the previous chapter in our analysis of man's fundamental structure we discovered that man is that existent thing who stands before the free God who may possibly reveal himself, and that he occupies this position through a deliberate (and even necessary) attitude to himself. Now we have just demonstrated that fundamentally this attitude to himself embraces an attitude to God. In order to follow out our anthropological analysis to its conclusion along this line, we must investigate the reciprocal relationship between desire and knowledge, the two inseparable factors in the one fundamental structure of human existence standing before God.

The disclosure of the transcendental horizon of being in general through which man stands before God takes place in a deliberate attitude which man adopts to himself. This is the human consequence and resultant of the free delimitation of

101

this finite cognitive existent thing by God. At the heart of knowledge is love, through which knowledge loves itself—though not in such a way, it is true, that knowledge is *preceded* by a blind urge, but in such a way that knowledge and love, first and last, constitute the one, ever-complete basic disposition of the one human existence. Neither factor can be comprehended unless it is comprehended as changing into the other, and as referring to the other.

All that we have done by this argument is to expound the content of the scholastic axiom: *"eus-verum-bonum convertuntur."* We might equally well say: *ens-intellectus-voluntas convertuntur.* In the end this would mean that knowledge and will, despite their distinction, are to be grasped conceptually, each according to its own nature, only as inner factors of the thing which is, insofar as it "is" being. Thus, for example, a thing is knowledge only to the extent that it is being. Being, however, is "some thing" only to the extent that it is grasped as will also, so that in the end as in the beginning, knowledge too is grasped only if translated into will, thus becoming perfected in its own nature in the ontological constitution of a thing which is. Thus will and knowledge can be grasped only in a *reciprocal* priority, not in a simple one-way relationship to each other, even though these two priorities are non-interchangeable.

This deliberate relationship which is implied by the spirit's openness has so far always been declared to be a *necessary* thing. Man always bears a necessary relation to himself and thus affirms himself in this dynamic of self-assertion. This necessity, however, requires more precise definition.

This deliberate self-delimitation, which occurs through transcendence over being in general, is necessary insofar as it is unavoidable. It must not be confused, however, with a blind, dead actuality, with a kind of metaphysical inertia. It is an *understanding.* Man affirms himself *as* something because his affirmation, even if only implicit, occurs consciously. This self-assertion may thus be necessary in its actuality without our having to say anything straightway about the concrete mode of this self-understanding. The necessity, as *conscious* self-un-

102

derstanding, is not of such a kind as to demand an *unequivocal* definition of the concrete mode of this self-understanding. Man necessarily understands himself somehow or other. *How* he in fact regards himself may, on the other hand, be a question concerning his original freedom. And again this does not occur in the sense that man is able to comprehend himself as though the mode of his self-understanding were completely at the mercy of his fancy. The necessity of his self-assertion already implies that he is bound by a concrete law which lays down how he must comprehend himself. All that we have said about man so far has been nothing except the explication of this law. This self-understanding in its mode of occurrence is an act of man's *freedom*. Now we must demonstrate why that is so.[1]

To the extent that the things which are presented to human cognition are grasped through the pre-concept against the horizon of being in general, they are recognized as objects of a subject who subsists in himself. To this extent, then, these objects are grasped as possible ends of a deliberate attitude, of an act of judgment in which the objects appear as good. In this way being itself is disclosed as desirable. Man is thus transcendent with respect to the absolute good which is absolute being —God. But this absolute good is not presented to begin with as object, but simply as the ultimate objective of the pre-concept, it is presented in knowledge as will. In scholastic terms, it is presented only as *"beatitudo in communi"* and not as an object. It is given merely as the condition of the possibility of comprehending some finite good. Just as the spirit, as knowledge in virtue of its transcendence with respect to absolute being, brushes aside the finite thing known as a thing in its finitude, and grasps itself as subsisting within itself, so also the knowing spirit, in its transcendence with respect to the absolute good, grasps the finitude of the particular good that is presented to it. It also grasps itself as a subject subsisting in itself, that is, as free, acting and standing apart from this good. In affirming a good

[1] On the comprehension of decision, see *Das Dynamische in der Kirche*, Freiburg, 1958, esp. pp. 74ff. See also J. B. Metz, "Entscheidung," in *Handbuch theologischer Grundbegriffe* I, pp. 281-288.

it is subject to a necessity and in that sense is not free only to the extent that the affirmation is part of the conditions of the necessary openness of the spirit to good in general. The openness of the spirit to good is the only thing that is affirmed of necessity *a priori*. In the presence of the particular good, insofar as it is grasped, man is free because it is always presented as finite (if not in fact affirmed necessarily as finite). Thus man is free also in face of the conditions of the possibility of his openness to good in general, this is made into a reflex knowledge of objects of knowledge. For example, in this way the possibility of suicide and of hatred of God become comprehensible although man once more implicitly affirms himself and absolute good as the condition of the possibility of such a negative attitude towards his own existence and towards the absolute good. Precisely as *objects* these are not the condition of the possibility, and hence man cannot be free with respect to them.[2]

What now, we must ask, is the relationship of this possibility of the free attitude to the good, or more precisely, to the necessary affirmation of the right order of the good which is implicitly contained in the notion of transcendence with respect to being and good and thus to the basic constitution of man? To begin with we may say that it consists not only in a logical agreement or disagreement between the necessarily affirmed right order of the good and that order which is contained in the free choice of this or that particular good. Certainly, some such thing is present and is the first thing which should be mentioned. The love of God which necessarily exists at the foundation of human life must be freely assessed and affirmed by man, or man's free attitude may logically contradict this basic love, just as a particular judgment may be in harmony with or may contradict the first law of being and thought. This is not all, however, nor in

[2] With this primarily gnoseologically oriented founding of the freedom of the finite spirit in the face of God, we do not claim to give an *adequate* enlightening of finite freedom before God. See "Die Freiheit in der Kirche," in *Schriften zur Theologie* II, Einsiedeln, 1955, pp. 95-114; "Würde und Freiheit des Menschen," in *ibid.*, pp. 247-277. See also J. B. Metz, "Freiheit," in *Handbuch theologischer Grundbegriffe* I, pp. 403-414.

the end is it the decisive thing. The free decision concerning the particular good *reacts,* as it were, upon the openness to the right order of the good itself, which is found in the foundation of existence. This connection is absolutely unavoidable. But because a free decision about a particular objective good is ultimately always a decision and a formation of the person himself (because in every decision man actually decides *about himself* and not about an action or a thing), man reacts upon himself in this decision and this controls the standards of the love which determines his own nature. As far as it lies within his power and as far as is possible at all, in his freely adopted attitude to the particular good and in his acceptance or rejection of it, he forms the standards of his possible future decisions. Not only does he take over the structural law of his love and hate, but freely lays down anew the right laws which he has always affirmed in accordance with ontological necessity, or lays down anew his own laws in contradiction of the true order of love. And because in this way he is not merely establishing a disconnected series of individual acts but in each act is constituting a law for his *whole* action and life, man does not therefore act simply well or ill, but he himself becomes good or evil.

Thus the true order of love is formed, an order that is always implicitly affirmed (called, in ancient times, *synteresis*). In man it is his own order of love. Man knows and acts in terms of this self-delimited order, according to that to which he has committed himself in free delimitation. Man always possesses the God-given order of his love only in unity with the freely delimited order of his love which he has constituted correctly or falsely by his free response to the particular good.

At this point we must recall once again that at the heart of transcendence in man with respect to God there occurs a deliberate attitude of man to himself, that love is thus the condition of the knowledge of God. It is true that this was affirmed in the first place of the necessary love for God that is always already given with human existence. Now it has appeared, however, that this necessary love in free-acting man is never given

105

merely as "pure" and intrinsic. It is always found in an act which is being constantly perfected in an historical synthesis with the freely delimited order of the love of man himself.[3]

This amounts to saying that the concrete transcendence of man with respect to God always contains hidden within it a free decision which is its interior make-up. Free decision is not merely a consequence of knowledge, but itself helps to determine that knowledge. This means that the most profound truth is also the most free. The truth of the knowledge of God, in the way in which one understands his God, always rests upon the order of his love or upon its disorder. It is not as though man first of all knew God in a *neutral* fashion, subsequently considering whether to adopt a loving or a hating attitude towards this God. Such a neutral knowledge,[4] such "objectivity," is a dangerous abstraction of the philosophers, or else it arises from the presupposition that the concrete order of love in man corresponds perfectly to the necessary order of love which ever remains implanted by God within the depths of human existence. The concrete knowledge of God is always determined from the start by the way in which man loves and treasures the things presented to him. Metaphysical knowledge certainly never grasps its object before it grasps itself. It knows it only from the transcendence of the subject and from the orientation of man towards this. For this reason, on the one hand such metaphysical knowledge cannot be orientated away from the object itself, and on the other hand it depends upon all of the factors which determine the concrete mode and character of this transcendence. Such knowledge is thereby no less rigorous, objective, and logical. In its essence it is at the same time an effort made by the whole person in free decision. Any alteration in knowledge is, in this context, always a "conversion" as well, not just an alteration of view or a fresh product of research. Thus each

---

[3] Because man never "finds himself" as a neutral subject in his reflexion, but "is found" always already in a subjectivity informed by its own freedom. On the thomistic interpretation of this concept, see J. B. Metz, "Befindlichkeit," in *LThK* II, pp. 102-104.

[4] For a treatment of this subject in a wider context, see "Was ist Häresie?", in *Schriften zur Theologie* V, Einsiedeln, 1962, pp. 527-576, esp. 553f.

man has the God who corresponds to his effort and the manner of that effort. He who loves matter more than spirit will worship matter as the absolute, as his God. He who centers his mind upon the life-force and makes it the center of his own nature will make a God of his belly—to use St. Paul's language. And so on . . . The truths which all men accept, those of mathematics for instance, are no more rigorously and certainly proved than those of a metaphysics of God. They are accepted by all merely because, belonging as they do to the most peripheral of human activity, that of space and number, they are never able to contradict the deliberate understanding of being through the method of free love. Metaphysical knowledge is capable of stricter and more necessary proof because it is constantly being necessarily affirmed in the foundations of existence. But this very affirmation will be able to become the object of a self-reflective knowledge only in the measure that this knowledge can penetrate into the structure of the love which man has placed within himself through his concrete actions. That one might convince a villain of a mathematical truth but not of a proof of God's existence is no indication of the strength of the one and the weakness of the other, but an indication of the degree to which a "proof" of God's existence demands an effort from man.

From this it also emerges that asceticism, in the sense of the readiness to submit to self-criticism of one's own order of love, and the readiness to judge this in terms of the necessary basic elements of the true order of love and to reorganize it better according to the growing light of deeper insight, is a profound factor of concrete philosophy in a true man. Philosophical activity in recent centuries has completely lost sight of the fact that a true philosopher must lead the religious life of the cloister.

What insights have we gained from all this to help us elaborate our philosophy of religion? We stated already that man is that existent thing who stands both before a free God and the as-yet-unfulfilled possibilities of his freedom. That is to say, he stands before the God of a possible revelation in the sense which we have already defined more precisely. And now it has further become clear that man's cognitive openness to this God of a possible revelation is always simultaneously and essentially an openness that is determined in its inner concrete structure by the free attitude of man.

Openness towards God has shown itself as a question of the moral self-determination of man. Knowledge of God is interior, if we enquire into it as a real phenomenon in real men; it is a moral or, better—because it is a matter of a decision in the face of God—a religious problem. We may, therefore, formulate the second proposition[5] of our metaphysical-religious-philosophical anthropology by saying that man is that existent thing who stands in free love before the God of a possible revelation. Man is attentive to the speech or the silence of God in the measure in which he opens himself in free love to this message of the speech or the silence of the God of revelation. He hears this message of the free God *only if* he has not restricted the absolute horizon of his openness to being in general by a perverted love, only if he has not removed in advance the possibility of the word of God addressing him as he pleases, of meeting him in the form he desires to assume. In all this we have merely been seeking to grasp philosophically what our Lord said: "He who does what is true comes to the light" (John 3, 21).

We still have to answer the question: where is the concrete place in which the free, possible act of revelation of God can encounter man who recognizes it in freedom? If man is that being who must always wait upon the free act of God, through which God desires to disclose himself, *where* in his existence must he seek so that he will meet this revelation should it happen or if it has already happened? These are the next questions that must concern us.

[5] See the corresponding first and third proposition on pp. 67 and 161, respectively.

PART FOUR

THE PLACE WHERE
THE FREE MESSAGE IS FOUND

9. THE QUESTION

We concluded the previous chapter by asking where must the man who listens for a possible free revelation by God stand, if he is truly to hear it? [1] Where must he stand should it actually proceed from God, or already have proceeded from God, as a *positive* self-disclosure of God? To what must man attune his ear if he is to hear the revelation that possibly may proceed from God, or if he is to encounter the silence of God? Does he listen for something in the depths of his own being? Does such a revelation occur within the pure inwardness of the spirit; in a rapture or ecstasy of the soul that is caught up and carried

[1] At this point we should be reminded of what was already said in chapter 1, note 8. The question as to the locus of a possible, positive revelation inquires after the limits of a categorical-verbal revelation. If the question is thus put to begin with, it is then not argued, but posited, that a revelation as real absolute self-revelation of God, in the way Christianity knows it to have taken place, without question concerns the *whole* man and thus in its first attempt implies *that* "revelation" (in the way that all things categorical imply their transcendental basis and constantly bring it into appearance) which is given in the heightening and enlightening through grace of the transcendence of man. If then, in what follows, certain interpretations of the locus of revelation are rejected, this is meant only in the sense that, *first,* a natural and unhistorical misunderstanding of this locus is rejected, and *second,* a restriction of the delimitation of the one and ever-whole revelation to the transcendence (through grace) of man alone is rejected as being a misunderstanding of the essence of man and thus structure of God's acting on man as well. How the theories touched upon in what follows are to be judged justly in a historical sense is not really our concern here. For such a judgment, at any rate, the here mentioned inner "transcendental difference" in the process of revelation between enlightenment by grace of human transcendence itself and its categorical self-explication in the historical word, must not be left out of consideration (even if it has not become sufficiently and explicitly thematic in such theories and remains implicit rather than stated).

out of the space and time of its "worldliness" into spheres beyond all appearances and images to a speechless thou-to-thou, of spirit-to-spirit? Or is the place of God's revelation the dark inwardness of a fundamental mood, of a feeling, in the infinite longing of which the infinite speaks? Where else in man might the place of a possible revelation of God be? It seems that there are many possibilities which might, on the surface, be considered as such a place. All philosophies of religion are in the end nothing but attempts to tell us *where* man must wait if he is to encounter God, where he may find God.

Does such an attempt make any sense at all? Can we in some measure determine in advance from whence God must come if he is to meet man? May man, on his own, determine the place where such a meeting is to take place? Does such an idea not already constitute a contradiction of what we have already discovered about God's being free, and so unpredictable to the mind of man? On the other hand, is not every indication of the "place" where God's revelation is obliged to take place an *a priori* law imposed by man upon such a revelation, insofar as the peculiarity of such a place of spiritual encounter already declares what sort of thing can happen there? Everything is not necessarily possible everywhere. Even if this were not so, if the indication of a place for such a positive revelation does not determine in advance the content and manner of such a free encounter between God and man, how can this place be determined at all? Is not every such determination an arbitrary preference of some human idiosyncrasy which is turned into the favored place of God's revelation?

A few things come to light already as a result of these tentative considerations.

(1) The "place" of a possible revelation by God may not be determined in such a way as to restrict the possibilities of such a revelation in advance. It may not be so conceived as to allow an *a priori* deduction concerning the *content* of such a free revelation by God.[2] In this case, the revelation would only be

---

[2] If the transcendence of man is posited as ever-enlightened by divine self-revelation (the most original moment of positive revelation), and if man encounters *this* transcendence in his historical experience, then

the objective correlative of the natural, non-historical religious structure of man himself. This is the basic error of every modernist philosophy of religion, whether it be conceived in a rationalist sense in which revelation is but another name for that which the non-historical autonomous spirit of man is able to know unaided about God, or conceived as feeling (in Schleiermacher's sense) of utter dependence, or again as the experience of the *mysterium tremendum et fascinosum* (Otto), or in any other way. Always and in every one of these cases the content of a possible "revelation" is defined in terms of a specific religious structure and experience; it is defined in a one-way direction, from man outwards, "from below"[3]; and then, starting from this

---

the revelation we mean here is of itself already "given" in its essential content as well. But in this case also the categorical objectivation and explication of the being of man is necessary, and not a "private" possibility presented to the whims of a single religious subject; for it happens precisely in what we call the one history of salvation and revelation as brought about by God, in which alone is attained the "revealedness" of revelation which is proper to and necessary for man. This necessarily categirical trait of the one revelation shows too that the history of revelation on the whole always bespeaks *genuinely human* history as well.

[3] The necessity of a categorical-historical objectivation of "transcendental revelation" (mentioned in notes 1 and 2 of the present chapter) also indicates that precisely this "transcendental revelation" is given to the ever-one and ever-whole human only *within* his categorical experience; it cannot be grasped in its pure transcendence and formality, so that the grasping of historical revelation would always remain an unavoidable afterthought but in the last analysis an inconsequential one. "Transcendental revelation," *as itself* is comprehended and becomes apparent only in its categorical concreteness, and this to such an extent in that it is only in the increasing involvement in this categorical history of revelation that its "transcendence" becomes increasingly apparent. The inner-historical-categorial exegesis of the revelation is at the same time the genuine history of its "transcendence." For "transcendental revelation" is not a "set" magnitude materially resting in itself, which would be objectivated anew in categorial chiffres in an *ex post facto*, if sometimes unavoidable manner; it much rather comes into its own reality in this categorial history of revelation, and must itself be understood to be "temporal"—just as in general the transcendental—*a priori* constitution of the human spirit may not in the last analysis be understood as a "set" magnitude, as a certain material "law," "with" which the spirit contemplates the aposteriori-categorial material, but in such a manner that the transcendental apriority of the spirit determines itself when it enters upon aposteriori-categorial reality, that is, that it itself comes to historical self-realization; only if understood thus, can it be divorced

standpoint, the content of a specific historical revelation is critically tested. It may be that certain elements are ruled out as irrelevant because they are considered not to be in harmony with, or at least not to be demanded by, the content that has been determined *a priori* as possible. We must reject such a view of the place of a possible revelation on the basis of the understanding we have already gained. Man is transcendent with respect to being in general. From this fact it is at once evident that he is directly open to being, so that either he already possesses it, and a revelation of what is already manifest is not possible, or precisely because of this absolute transcendence he cannot by his own capacity possess a preliminary law of that which can and is to be revealed. He who is essentially open to being cannot by his own capacities set limits to the possible object of a revelation. He must keep himself open to being in general. Because man is not absolute "having being," only the second supposition remains; for any spirit, by reason of its unlimited transcendence, the place of a possible revelation contains no *a priori* law governing the possibilities of that which is to be revealed.

(2) The categorical disclosure of any unknown being may proceed intrinsically in two ways, either by the presentation of the one to be disclosed in his own self, or by the mediation of a knowledge of him through the word. By "word" we mean primarily a representative symbol of him who is not presented in person. To the extent that man is absolute openness of the spirit with respect to being in general (that is, to absolute being), the possibilities of a revelation by self-presentation of the one

---

from a pure formality on the one hand, without thereby having to become an unhistorical, material law of the spirit that has always been defined—in the sense of a bad, unhistorical and material apriority or ending as a purely *aposteriori* result. To put it differently: the historicity of the human spirit does not finally consist simply in the fact that its transcendental apriority is formally relegated to the facts of an *a posteriori* world, but in that this being-relegated itself has a *substantial* meaning for the regaining of consciousness of the human spirit, that the content of the transcendental self-experience of the human spirit, and that, inversely, the transcendental self-experience thus understood and consummated reveals itself to be the true "facticity" and apriority—the one underivable history of the human spirit.

to be revealed are not exhausted until man sees the absolute
God directly in his own self. As long as God does not disclose
his own self *directly* to man, man must always count on the
possibility of a revelation of this God in the *word* in the sense
just defined. As long, therefore, as man has not attained a share
in the direct vision of God, as long as he is a listener to the
word of God, in virtue of the basic constitution of his existence,
he is the one who has to count on a possible revelation of God
that consists not in the direct presentation of him who is to be
revealed, but in his self-imparting through the mediation of a
representative symbol, through the pointing of another being to
the one who is to be revealed.[4]

(3) This place cannot be determined in advance in such a
way as to designate a specific part of man's basic constitution
as the sole favored place of such a revelation. God can reveal
only what man is able to hear. This proposition is at once
obvious. That this proposition does not imply any preliminary
limitation of possible objects of a revelation has already become
clear from the establishment of the transcendence of the human
spirit with respect to being in general. To this extent it is also
obvious that absolute openness to being must be an interior
factor of this place of a possible revelation. If we were to modify
the proposition, however, and say, "God is able to reveal only
what man can perceive through this or that structure of his
nature, through this or that basic experience, through this or
that religious sentiment, through this or that religious experience," then the unlimited openness of the spirit and also the
freedom and incalculability of a possible revelation of God
would be annulled.

Nonetheless, the place of the possible revelation of God has
still not been unambiguously defined by saying that it is the
unlimited possibility of man, opened up by the transcendence of
the spirit, to perceive every word which proceeds from the

[4] How (of course exclusively in connection with the enlightened-by-
grace subjectivity of man) such a representative categorial sign ("word")
can nevertheless in a true sense be the presence of real divine self-
revelation, and how this sign ("word") as a *human* one does not depo-
tentiate this word of God in the first place to the level of a mere human
knowledge, is not a question we are here concerned with.

115

mouth of God. For this transcendence itself has still not been adequately described. It has not, indeed, yet been grasped in its specifically *human* character. It has just been stated that the place of a possible revelation can be defined only by saying that man *as man* is this place. If now we are to define this place more precisely we will always have in mind the character of human transcendence. What we must think of are the characteristics of human transcendence and not something that is different from it. And so our task is to define more extensively the nature of man himself, going beyond our previous abstract statement that he is finite spirit.

From general ontology it has already appeared that there is a certain historical character about a possible revelation. When he is known as the existent thing with absolute "having being," God stands before man as the one who acts freely, who has not yet exhausted the possibilities of his freedom towards finite man through the free delimitation of this finite thing. But free action is in an essential sense historical action. An initial general and metaphysical understanding of history shows it always to exist where free delimitation exists. It is a happening that cannot be deduced and calculated from a general preceding cause. Such a free non-derivable happening is always a unique, unrepeatable something, to be understood in terms of itself alone. It is not merely one case of a general law. An historical event stands in contrast to a datum of natural scientific knowledge which is a particular expression of a necessary and general law that exhaustively explains the case. Thus we contrast an historical event with a natural event. Thus, from God's angle, revelation displays itself as an historical phenomenon.[5]

[5] Compare, however, chapter 6, note 3, where it is indicated that revelation can and must show itself to be an historical occurrence in relation to man, and this because already the self-comprehension of man as a *creature* (and thus as an existence continually dependent on God) consists in that man accepts himself in his standing before the God of inevitable and inexhaustible freedom and in this sense already has a "history with God" in his creaturely self-comprehension, that is, an inevitable relationship to divine freedom, which would finally act upon man in an historical sense, that is, actively dispose over him, if it continually kept to itself, because for God (as "pure act") this keeping-to-himself is also an original, active disposing underivable from man.

This briefly sketched concept of the historical is, however, no adequate description of that which constitutes the historical in *human* history. When we say that revelation is an historical process because it is the locale of any possible revelation we do not mean history in the general metaphysical sense, but in the sense of *human* history. What human history is will not be simply defined, but will appear out of the demonstration of man's historical character in the midst of his transcendence. This historical character of man is not to be demonstrated by a mere empirical proof, by a mere collecting of concrete actualities as they appear, but is to be grasped as part of man's basic constitution. As long as this was not done it would still be conceivable that man might think that he was capable, in virtue of his spirituality, of the attempt to raise himself as spirit above his history, to emancipate himself from it and so from the start to exclude history as a possible place of revelation for him. As spirit, he has the basic possibility of attempting this feat, but not of achieving it. It has to be demonstrated, therefore, that the importance of the historical setting for revelation is an inner factor in the spirituality of man himself. If we achieve this we will have demonstrated also that the place of a possible revelation of God, that is, of man's openness to being in general, lies necessarily *within* human history.[6]

Therefore, the question before us is: how does the *spiritual* nature of man, in his historical context, arise out of his fundamentally constituted transcendental make-up? Note that man is not an historical character *de facto* but he becomes one by his openness to the transcendent, that is, to God. It is quite obvious that such an undertaking can be initiated only where man's transcendence has demonstrated itself as a result of the general

---

[6] Again we must basically observe that in the same way that the human spirit comes into its own reality only in the turning to history, the opposite is also true: history as it is here understood, is not already adequately constituted in itself *before* the (necessary) turning of the human spirit to it, but it has its birth first and foremost as true human history in this turning towards it. The *conversio* of the spirit, then, belongs to the constitution of this history, to its historicity as such; and the substantial determination of this history cannot be separated from the factual material self-development of the human spirit. See above, note 3.

enquiry into being. After we have analyzed what this implies concerning the basic constitution of man, we must make yet a third fresh attempt at analysis. At the beginning of this study we described the *third aspect* under which the problem of being must be considered: man must enquire about being in general in such a fashion that he enquires about the being of a *thing which is,* that is, distinguishing between being and the existent thing.

It has been stated earlier that the most general question about being is only the most general formalization of every judgment presented in the form of a question. Such a judgment is of necessity made every time a man thinks or acts. Every proposition says something about something for example "The cat is black." Or, more generally, this (existent thing) has this (particular) kind of being. Such a proposition as is obvious, is but the formal affirmative answer to the general problem of being under the particular aspect in which we now meet it. "What kind of a being is this existent thing?" It is in these terms that we have to ask: what conclusion can we draw for our purpose from the analysis of this proposition? The proposition may equally well be expressed in the form of a question or in the form of a statement. Insofar as this proposition always occurs in man's life in the concrete, the conclusion of this analysis, implicitly affirmed in the proposition, can also be explicitly affirmed.

However, before we are able to proceed directly with this analysis of our problem of being we must first recall a previous conclusion, and make a statement.

The previous conclusion is this: being is being-present-to-itself. This we concluded earlier from the analysis of the general problem of being. This means, as we said earlier, that cognition in its first and original concept is not some kind of grasping of an object or the deliberate putting of oneself into a relationship with something else. But it is the self-presence of an existent thing being reflected in one's own being and the attribution of "having being" that is thus recognized by this act. In the same context we stressed that this "having being" is an analogy, a concept that varies interiorly in its meaning. A metaphysical understanding of a specific existent thing (man, for example)

118

is accordingly possible only by means of this original metaphysical concept of knowledge. This involves the grasping of the inner analogical variation which this concept of knowledge along with the analogy of "having being" (and vice versa) experiences.

The *statement* [7] that we have to make is this. Human knowing is *receptive* knowing. We speak at first simply of human knowing without making any distinction between possible different capacities for knowledge in man. For even though such differing capacities for knowledge in one particular man be grasped metaphysically, this cannot be done through a retrospective adding up of such capacities. Because unity always precedes multiplicity, it can be grasped only in such a way that the totality of all such capacities is grasped as original emerging out of the necessary unity which is the unfolding of the single nature of a man. It is of this single knowing of man that we make the assertion to begin with that human knowing is receptive knowing. That is to say, man is not antecedently in possession of his knowledge in virtue of his nature, but he has knowledge only inasmuch as an object displays itself to him of its own accord. It is not as if there were an obvious property which must be attached automatically to every cognition. It is the cognition of the angel, to take an example from Thomistic epistemology, which is founded upon its being present to itself through itself alone. His own nature is originally illumined by himself and for himself without his requiring the grasping of any other thing differentiated from himself in order to make the act of knowledge present to himself. With man the reverse is true. He is present to himself only while he grasps another object that is different from himself, an object that must contact him and show itself to him as being which is distinct from him. This being present to himself, the reflection of being in himself which constitutes the essence of the cognition, is possible to man only through an outgoing to another existent thing that is different from him. In anticipation of further discussion we may

[7] The following chapter (10) will reveal, in the natural course of its development, that what seems here at first to be the simple determination of a fact originally stems from a transcendental necessity.

119

say now that in the case of man, "return to oneself" is always a "going out into the world" and is effected through it. And so, when man turns towards something outside himself desiring to know it, he is not assuming control over a cognition that is already completely established within his own essence. If we once accept this formulation of the receptivity of human knowledge and follow it out logically, it can be concluded from this alone that man is never able to detach himself from a starting point of his whole knowledge which is outside himself. This external origin of all his knowledge must appear in every act of his cognition. All advance in knowledge remains for ever essentially attached to the original starting point. It is in fact nothing but the unfolding of this original datum. If, then, human knowledge is essentially receptive knowledge, the basic structure of knowledge of the thing initially received and the way it is received will persist throughout all subsequent acts of knowledge and determine the structure of human knowledge in general. Every return within oneself will always display the fact that human knowledge can be grasped only by a going out into the world. Our task, therefore, will be to define more exactly the metaphysical structure of this starting point. By "starting point" we mean both the receptive capacity for and also the object as such, initially grasped. The two form a profound unity because knowing and the thing known in virtue of their original unity in being-as-such, correspond to one another, and hence a specific receptive cognition must have an interior correspondence to its own determining object (in our case, the original thing capable of being received).

We have discovered—so we believe—the object of our enquiry and where we must look to find the answer. We are seeking to find the place of encounter between man and the God who may possibly reveal himself. This place is the transcendence of man in its specifically *human* character. The answer to our question begins once again with the most general question about being. We consider this under its third aspect: we enquire about being, distinguishing between being and the existent thing. A presupposition of this distinction is the fact that man is a receptive knower. In what follows we will have to start from this receptive knowledge and the conditions of its possibility.

120

10. MAN AS A MATERIAL ESSENCE

We are asking what kind of place it must be in which a possible revelation of God to man takes place. The question is understood in this sense: we are enquiring about the character of human *transcendence*. This character is intended to indicate to us under the *third* aspect of the general problem of being, the original distinction between being and the existent thing, a distinction that is necessary for man. In order to proceed beyond this starting point we had in the previous chapter to recall something and to make a statement. We recalled that being is being-present-to-itself, and that in its origin knowing is nothing other than the being-present-to-itself of the existent thing to the extent of its "having being." We stated that human knowing, that is, being-present-to-oneself in a return into oneself, is possible only as a receiving through going out to something other than oneself that is grasped objectively as the first object of knowledge.

This recollection of previous considerations and this statement seem to have led us into a contradiction. For knowing, in its specific metaphysical essence, is supposed to be the being-present-to-itself of the already existent knowing subject. Thus understood, the concept of an original receptive knowledge seems to be an absurdity. It is true that our basic concept of knowledge makes it readily evident that something differentiated from the knower can also be known. When, for example, an existent thing grasps itself, when it knows, from its own essence, all of its various aspects, then it is able to grasp itself as the cause and creative basis of something other than itself, and thus know this other thing in its being present to itself as a possible object of its own causality. In this way, God, for example, knows things that are other than himself. As absolute being he

121

is present to himself from all eternity and grasps his own essence in the reflection in itself of his absolute "having being." Hence he knows himself also as the almighty creative cause of finite existent things and thus knows these things themselves. The difficulty created by this original concept of the possibility of knowing something other than oneself arises only if we presuppose that this other thing reacts to the knower as some other constitutive cause of "having oneself." If being denotes being present to oneself, and knowing is nothing other than the being-present-to-itself of the existent thing, then from the very start it would seem that the cause of the knowledge of a knowing subject must always be its *own essence*. In our statement we put forward the proposition that human knowledge is a receptive knowledge in the sense that its initial cause is something other than self and differentiated from self. Here we seem to be saying that man is present to himself only when he reaches out to another being, knowing himself in doing so, letting himself be met by this other thing, and thus being able to achieve a return into himself only through an outgoing into a world that is differentiated from himself. How can we resolve this incongruity?

What was said earlier about the analogy of these concepts shows that such a question is possible. We mean that the concepts that we use in our question, being and knowing, are not unambiguous fixed entities in the question itself, turning the question into a self-contradiction. To begin with, we answer this question quite formally, saying that the being of any existent being must be being which has its origin outside itself. If we put forward this proposition quite specifically at the outset, the lack of harmony which we have just tried to express is resolved. If the knower possesses his being as that of another, it is obvious that if through knowledge this being is present to itself, it is also knowingly present to the other as the being of which the knower "has" his being. If this existent thing has its being as that of another, then his being reflected in himself is primarily and not just secondarily the being reflected in itself of this other thing. That which is first known in this being reflected in oneself is then the other being in which the knower was already present himself—ontologically and not only through the knowledge as such. Yet we still have to explain the meaning of this very formal and abstract talk of an ontological being being present to another being, and through this being present to oneself and thus naturally turning into a cognitive being present to some other being. More precision is needed.

In order to resolve the contradiction between the basic constitution of knowledge in general and the receptivity of human knowledge we said that being as the being of man, as being itself present to something else, should be the being of another. We do not say "being," but "existent thing," because our statement about the luminosity of an existent thing was made with reference to the extent in which it "has" being, that is, to the extent to which luminosity is attributed to the "having being" of the existent thing. For that reason the being of man is to be understood as an ontological being present to something else. It is obvious that this mysterious "something else," grasped so far only formally, cannot itself be being. Otherwise, it could not contribute to the resolution of the difficulty which we find in the notion of the reflection in oneself of being itself. It is this reflection which raises the possibility of having another being present to oneself as the thing first known. Accordingly, this "something else" must be a real thing and yet not be being, as such, not something known in itself. If it were it would have to be reflected in itself, thus be the cause of the knowledge of *itself,* and not the cause of the knowledge of "something else." This "something else" is thus the *subjective possibility* of "having being," which on the one hand is real [1] and really distinct from the being (of the "actuality"), and yet on the other hand "as

[1] The "reality" of this subject-like "possibility" may of course not be understood as one that belongs to it positively and so to speak independently of the being that comes towards it. The concept of "reality" does not admit of being thought of without referral to "being" if it is not to be simply another term for "being." The reality of this "possibility" then, must not be thought of as constituted by being itself, inasmuch as being, in its ontological "future" ("coming towards") postulates for itself this subject-like possibility of having-being. Actually, here the formal basic problematic of all metaphysics appears once again, in that the difference in comprehension of unity must continually be present and that difference does not repeal unity even as last unity, but constitutes it.

sheer possibility" is not an existent thing which must intrinsically be self-consciously present to itself. That is, it is not itself in a state of actual "having being." Accordingly, man's being is the being of an empty, unspecific, subjective possibility of being that is really distinct from actual "having being." The term for this concept in Thomistic metaphysics is *"materia."* [2] As already appears from its derivation, this concept has nothing whatever to do with the modern concept of a physical or chemical matter. The matter of chemistry is a *thing* that somehow is subject to the observation of natural science at least. The *materia* of Thomistic ontology is indeed a real metaphysical constituent of an existent thing, but it is not observable, it is not to be concerned as material. We cannot imagine the real, subjective possibility of an existent thing—really distinct from being, yet presupposed by being itself—as some kind of physical ultimate corpuscle or some kind of ether. It is, so to speak, a postulate of metaphysics, not, it is true, in the sense of a natural scientific hypothesis, but in the sense of a metaphysical principle, of a something that as such can never be the object of natural scientific observation (for one can observe only things, not metaphysical principles of things), but which is rigorously and necessarily demanded for metaphysical reasons.

The being of man that the scholastics call *forma* is thus the "having being" of that unspecified real possibility that is called *materia.* The being of man is actualized in itself in such a way that even in its first incipient essence it must be comprehended as the reality of the "other," that is, of the *materia.* (Why it

[2] It must be admitted that the exegesis of the ontological difference in its incompleteness (and this is our point of departure) as concerns *materia prima* has not been adequately followed through here; for example, it must remain unclear whether final cognition, that is, cognition in incomplete ontological difference, and accepting cognition are necessarily the same thing or not. In the first case the problem of incomplete ontological difference would be materially identical with what is treated in scholastic philosophy under the heading of *materia prima.* Whichever the case may be, we nevertheless have the right to make an exposition of the problem of incomplete ontological difference in relation to the problem of *materia prima,* because the concreteness of the ontological difference that we have in fact experienced is that of accepting, worldly cognition, and because transcendental formalities can be determined only and alone on the basis of their *a posteriori* concreteness.

must be said to be actualized in itself will be specially discussed later.) Let us stress once again the fact that we have established a part of the human ontological basic constitution that does not merely belong accidentally to man (as if his essence could be put together retrospectively out of pieces), but we have deduced this part of his essential constitution from the first account we gave of human knowledge. What we have been expounding so far is nothing other than the Thomistic proposition, *"Anima humana est forma corporis,"* wherein we understand *"corpus"* in the Thomistic sense as *materia prima,* as the empty real possibility of being.[3]

Naturally, this is but a very unpolished account of the problems which explicitly affect us here. Now we must enquire more precisely what exactly is this *materia* which has been posited as the metaphysical presupposition of human knowledge. Also, how this account of man's being makes a receptive knowledge metaphysically comprehensible must be made at least a little clearer. In all of these researches we must never be allowed to forget what was said at the very beginning of our discussion, namely, on the one hand, that we are able to talk about the philosophy of religion only if we allow it to build itself up from the foundation and do not speak *about* it as though we knew in advance what it was; and on the other hand, that in a few pages we are able to give only the roughest sketch of this subject which is really general metaphysics. In these circumstances, we are left with the consolation that at least we are indicating for those who are already acquainted with Thomistic metaphysics how a philosophy of religion must work itself out within a Thomistic framework. For those who are still unacquainted with this metaphysics, we are giving some inkling of what it contains. We cannot be expected to do more than this.

We stand now, therefore, at a fresh point of departure for our insight into the constitution of man's being. Man is receptive knowledge of such a kind that his self-comprehension or his conscious being-present-to-himself always derives basically from a movement out towards the world. It derives from the grasping

---

[3] For an extensive treatment, see *Spirit in the World,* pp. 325ff.

of something distinct from himself, that is, the initially grasped object of human knowledge in general. From this was deduced the proposition that man is and must be an existent thing whose being (ontological reality) is the being of an empty possibility of being that is different from himself. Now we must set about expounding this proposition more precisely.

To the extent that we derive this insight from an epistemological argument it is obvious that this insight applies to man just to the extent that he is receptively cognitive. In other words, man, as receptive knower and insofar as his knowledge is the reception of an object and not the *a priori* possession of an innate knowledge, is the being of *materia*. Knowledge of such a nature is the being of a real, completely unspecified possibility of being that is distinct from it itself. It is the *materia* on which the actual knowledge of a material subject is based. It is knowledge through the senses. That is to say, receptive knowledge, in the sense which we have frequently defined, is essentially *sense perception*. We have thus arrived at a *metaphysical* concept of human sense perception. We are not here describing an *a posteriori* description of the concrete form of this sense perception. Such a description would have to proceed from the particular sense faculties. Not only have we ascertained that sense perception is an actually emergent faculty of perception in man, but have also recognized that reality is to be sensuously perceived by reason of the metaphysically required nature of receptive knowledge, and hence conversely have grasped the metaphysical nature of sense perception. Sense perception is the knowledge possessed by that existent thing which, in order to possess anything other than itself as its initially given object, must itself be the being of the *materia*.

Now we have to answer the question: how can the nature of this *materia,* in which the being of the sensuously receptive knower subsists, be made clearer? In answering this question the nature of man as a sensuously receptive knower will also become more precisely understandable.

We will set about answering this question by asking a preliminary question. What must the metaphysical structure of that existent thing be which is the initial *object* of a receptive cognition? If knowing is originally the act of being present to itself of an existent thing then we can also say: the ontological structure of a knowing creature is the *a priori* law of its possible objects of knowledge. The structure of an existent thing possessing a specific "having being" can be translated into the structure of the act of its being present to itself, and hence into the structure of its initially grasped object of knowledge as such. If being-present-to-itself and knowing are the being-present-to-itself of the existent thing as a mode of its "having being," then the thing initially known is always the specific "being" of the knower himself. Thus the structure of the knower as an existent thing is the structure of the thing known, and vice versa. If the thing initially known is something other than oneself, but if it is so precisely because the being of the knower is the being of the other, then the structure of the knower as an existent thing is the structure of the thing known. That is to say, if the being of the sensuously receptive knower is the being of the *materia,* then the thing known must itself be material in the same sense. We might say, therefore, that the original object of a receptive cognition can only be the being that is founded in *materia* as its reality.

At this point we may refer back explicitly to the third aspect of our general problem of being. We always grasp being *objectively* as that of an existent thing. We grasp it as something which is the answer to the question: what is this existent thing? [4] Thus we distinguish, as we see from our general formulation of the problem of being, between a *forma* and a *subiectum,* between an essence and its subject. We never possess an object as present in our knowledge except in the way that is characterized by this distinction. This *subiectum,* of which the answer to the question "What is it?" is conceived to be the substantial determination, cannot now be being *in itself.* For as such it would have to be *of itself* a comprehensible, self-luminous act

---

[4] We here say "existingness," first in order to place the proposition determined in terms of quiddity in contrast to a particular existent; in the second place, in order to emphasize that this material contemplation of the being of an existent no longer sees this being essentially on the plane of the continuing happening of the ontological difference, but in the dimension of the ontic neuter and of quidditative predication.

of existing. Thus it would itself be expressible as *"quidditas"* or "thisness" and once again would have to be referred to another *subiectum*. This determination towards something else of the act of existing can only be the empty and unspecified subjective possibility of "having being." Thus so from the standpoint of the way in which humans grasp an existent thing we once again stand before the same *materia* as we found previously. But approaching it from this new angle we are in a better position to say what it is. It appeared as the empty, non-specific determination towards something other than self of the act of being of an existent thing which became intelligible when referred to this very *materia*. This *"quidditas"* always appears in the judgment where it supplies the content of the predicate of the proposition, and the *materia* appears as the non-specific subject which in itself could be any of various possible answers to the question "What is it?" In this lack of specification the *materia* shows itself as the receiving cause which provides the possibility of allowing the question "What is it?" to be asked and answered. And so, as the final term of a predication, the *materia* is the cause of the act of existence of an existent thing, the "thisness" of which is, on this basis, in itself repeatable. In this way, the *materia* is the *principium individuationis,* not in the sense of an individuality which, through the complete and total possession of the act of "having being" would be absolutely unrepeatable, but in the sense of an individuality that is proper to an existent thing. *Materia* is thus the *principium individuationis,* not in the sense of being the cause of a specific unique thing, but in the sense of the cause of any particular realization of a thing.[5] This definition of *materia* enables us to gain further insights both into the nature of man and also into the nature

[5] This is not meant to be an adequate piece of information about *materia* as the *principium individuationis;* in relation to the problem of the "one" *materia* (see *Spirit in the World,* pp. 345ff.) one could also pose, even under the preceding conditions, the problem of the unrepeatability of the one material world as a whole, and *materia* could also be understood as the sufficient reason for the unrepeatable uniqueness of the history of free persons, so that from these two aspects, the *materia* as the *principium individuationis* yet attains a positive meaning for the uniqueness in the sense of the quidditative unrepeatability.

of the object which he is able to possess by his act of knowledge.

At all events, one thing has long since become clear: to say that man is spirit is to say that he participates in being-outside-himself, and is always in this state of having entered existentially into the *materia* and thus into the world. This definition is not a statement added to that about his spirituality, but a profound definition of his spirituality itself. Obviously, this is not meant to be taken in a sense that would make spirituality a *special* sensate capacity of man. Such a statement would contain an inner contradiction. It is meant to be taken in the sense that man as a receptive spirit, by his very human nature (*anima tabula rasa*), required a sensuous faculty as his own necessary means to attain his goal, the comprehension of being in general. In this sense man is sensate spirituality. The *anima intellectiva,* that is, the spirit, is *vere et essentialiter corpus informans,* to use the language of the Council of Vienne.[6] The soul as spirit of itself (*"per se"*) goes out into *materia.* We have already discovered a point of departure on the way to finding out how this is to be understood. *Materia* is *principium individuationis.* Beginning with that, we must continue our enquiry until we discover what it means to say that man, precisely as spirit, lives in this world.

[6] Denzinger, 481.

11. MAN AS HISTORICAL SPIRIT

Anima forma materia. The previous chapter was meant to be a first demonstration of this proposition. At the same time a starting point has emerged from which we may proceed to understand *materia prima.* It is the empty, non-specific, although real possibility of "having being," and as such is the cause of its manifold actualization. It has already been stated likewise that by such a definition of the nature of a material existent thing a statement is made both concerning man as receptive knower, and also about the original object as that which shows itself, of itself, to a receptive intelligence.

Arising from this concept of the *materia* two further definitions can be made concerning the *materia.* It is the cause of *space* and *time.*

It is the cause of the spatiality of an existent thing. The "thisness" of the object of our knowledge appeared intrinsically as universal, that is, as something which in itself is undetermined, as the specification of any particular thing. This universal may come to subsist with *materia* as its subject any indeterminate number of times. If such a *forma,* such a "thisness," actually subsists repeatedly in the *materia* and thus the same thing is frequently repeated, there arises the possibility of adding up these same things. Number is possible only where that which is supposed to be capable of addition appears *a priori* as the repetition of the same thing. And as the *materia* displayed itself as the principle of the possible repetition of the same thing, we must necessarily posit it as the principle of number. But where number is, there is quantity. *Materia* is the principle of quantity, for this is nothing other than the quantitative repetition of the same thing. *Materia* is such a principle not merely in respect of several

130

existent things that are really distinct from one another, but it must also necessarily exercise its essential function within the particular existent thing by entering into it as essential principle. But this means that it constitutes the particular existent thing as quantitative *in itself*. The repetition of the same thing within one single existent thing is nothing less than its own spatiality, its intrinsic "quantumness," the real differentiation of the same thing within the unity of an existent thing. We can say, therefore, that wherever an existent thing in virtue of the constitution of its being has *materia* for its intrinsic essential principle, it is spatial.

A further basic specification of a material existent thing is its intrinsic temporality. *Materia* appeared as the intrinsically non-specific possibility of "existentness." At the same time, however, it always displays itself as *wider* than that particular "existentness" of which it is the subject in this or that particular existent thing. The particular *"quidditas"* which is rooted in the *materia* does not fill up its full extent. Hence, in virtue of the ever greater extent and unfilledness of its *materia,* a material existent thing is always leaning towards new self-particularizations. It is ever on the move towards the attribution of fresh particularizations in the future. These particularizations are already revealed in the foundation of the essence of the existent thing through the non-specific breadth of the *materia* and its possibilities. The material existent thing is thus that existent thing which has ahead of it the sum total of the realization of its possibilities always as that which is yet to come from its own inner activity towards which it is moving. Insofar as these possible particularizations, which might equally be the realization of the unlimited possibilities of the *materia,* are excluded at least in part as simultaneous particularizations of the same *materia,* the totality of possible realizations of the potentiality of the *materia* as such always remains unfulfilled, that is, it is never there all at once. The totality of the actualization of the possibilities of a material existent thing is realizable only in the sequence of the inner activity of this existent thing. That is to say, the existent thing is in time. Temporality is here taken in its original meaning, not as the external measure of duration of the presence of an existent thing, but as the inner extension of the existent thing itself into the actualized totality of its possibilities. These could not all at once particularize that existent thing. Each particularization, as "this" sort of *materia,* is of itself dynamically orientated towards something else by which it itself is annihilated. And so we must affirm that a material existent thing is intrinsically temporal. By this we have gained three definitions of *materia.* It is the cause of the actual repeatability of the same thing. It supplies the existent thing, of which it is the essential element, with an interior spatiality and an interior temporality.

What we have now to do, therefore, is to make use of the deepened insight which we have acquired into the nature of the *materia* in order to help us gain a metaphysical concept of man. A man is one among many. In terms of his nature a man exists in time and space. Insofar as his *"quidditas"* is intrinsically that of *materia,* he "has-a-being" that is intrinsically repeatable. The individual man is fundamentally one of a race. Obviously, we are not going to attempt here[1] to prove the fact of a biological link through generation or even the concrete mode of such a biological link by *a priori* metaphysical deduction. There is one thing, however, that may well be open to *a priori* metaphysical illumination. Man, in virtue of his essential constitution as a material essence in its *"quidditas,"* is repeatable. That is, there can be *many* men. This is to say also that even on the assumption that in fact there was only one man, this one man would be bound to possess an intrinsic relationship to a possible multiplicity of those like himself. In the exposition of the temporality of a material existent thing it has already been stressed that a particular material thing is never able all at once to realize the never-ending extent of the possibilities which lie enclosed within its materiality. This fact makes evident also that an individual man is never able, totally, to realize the possibilities that are proper to him by reason of his material essence as a particular

[1] For the attempt at a transcendental deduction of the racial unity of mankind see "Theological Reflexions on Monogenism," in *Theological Investigations,* London and Baltimore, 1961, Vol. I, especially pp. 286-296.

individual. Consequently, the indication which each man bears in himself that there are other such beings is not an irrelevance, but a pointer to the existence of a human race which can manifest only in its totality the essence that is granted to each individual man in the foundation of his potentialities as such. Man is real only as a part of humanity.[2]

The significance of the fact that man as material essence is spatial and temporal is surely self-evident. Man is not merely set within a space-time world as an adjunct to his essential constitution. It is not as though he were later set upon a space-time stage where he may act a part. Space-time is his interior specific constitution. Because *materia* is his essential element, space and time arise out of himself as interior factors of his existence.

If we say that man is essentially one of many of the same kind with whom he is thrown together in time and space by reason of his interior essence, then we are saying only that he is historical in the concrete sense of a *human* history. At an earlier stage in our study we already attributed to man's action a historicity that is genuine and necessary, but this has also a wider meaning. Man is historical insofar as he is the one who acts in a freedom that originates in his transcendence with respect to God, that is, according to the determination of his relationship to the absolute. Obviously, this factor belongs essentially to the historicity of man. Genuine historicity is there only where we find the uniqueness and unpredictability of freedom. Nature does indeed show variations and suffers activation, but it has no real history, because all the phases of its activity, even though not always reversible in direction, are but necessary factors and consequences of the initial configuration and thus merely cases

[2] This derivation of humanity as the personal "co-world" of man could be presented more precisely and in more concrete detail. But even then the point of departure would have to be man as a material being; yet it could be demonstrated that the "object" of an accepting cognition, if it is in truth to mediate a substantially filled being-with-itself, must be not just "the other," but "*the* (personal) other." Thus the transcendental constitution of being-with and co-world would appear just as original as that of the (material) *surrounding* world, in other words, "world" would become visible as the one common "corporeality" and thus as the domain of the mutual exchange and mutual dismissal of free historical existences.

of a universal law. History appears only where uniqueness and individual worth triumph over fortuitousness and value of position, in other words where there is freedom. In the *human* sense, historicity is found only where the act of freedom spreads out within the context of free persons in their diversity in a space-time world. Historicity is found only where the intelligible acts of freedom necessarily extend in space and time, that is, where they require space-time in order to become themselves. It is this sort of historicity which appears in man in virtue of his essential constitution. This is the historicity of a free person who subsists in himself, who within a society of persons like himself experiences the total realization of this personal essence in space and time. Man is an historical creature. Now this is no longer a mere assertion, made as the result of an addition of disparate actualities and their retrospective integration. It is an insight into man's nature. The factors that go to make up the original account of this nature are now being grasped in their necessary sequence and context.

Before we place this knowledge in direct relationship to our question in the field of the philosophy of religion, a few additional observations have still to be made, to fill out our argument so far. The first observation concerns the connection of our research with the propositions of Thomistic ontology. Those who are familiar with this will have no hesitation in granting that our deduction corresponds to this ontology. We proceed from the fact that human cognition is receptive. This is a basic viewpoint of Thomistic epistemology, which it shares with that of Aristotle. *Anima tabula rasa.* All of our ideas originate in a stimulus from the sensible world. St. Thomas rejects not only innate ideas but another kind of objective *a priorism* in knowledge also—the contemplation of ideas in the Augustinian sense. For such a contemplation would impart to man an objective knowledge that would be in origin independent of his sense perception and would be added to its constitution only retrospectively, as the norm of the world of sense perception. From the receptive character of our human knowledge, through a transcendental deduction, we arrived at the concept of cognition through the senses, and of *materia*. It is true that St. Thomas

134

had other ways that lead to the formation of the concept of the *materia;* but he knows this one, too. He speaks explicitly of a *via praedicationis*[3] by which man arrives at receptive knowledge of the *materia*. It could also be shown that for St. Thomas receptive knowledge and sense perception are strictly the same in essence. The proof could be carried out in various ways. For example, it could be achieved from the Thomistic metaphysic of the knowledge of the angels (insofar as these, being non-material creatures, cannot possess receptive knowledge), if our thesis is correct. We could thus show that, by our reasoning, according to St. Thomas, the knowledge which the angels[4] have of the things that are distinct from themselves must be conceived not as receptive knowledge (that is, knowledge deriving its content from the things themselves), but as knowledge produced through innate ideas and by participation in the active knowledge of God, and so is itself *scientia quasi activa*. Another way leading to the same thesis would be provided by showing that for St. Thomas an intra-mundane real-ontological influence of one existent thing upon another—which is the pre-condition of receptive knowledge—is possible only among material existent things. Here we must be content with these pointers.[5]

If the materiality of the human existent thing is conceived as something that knows itself in the receptive knowledge of things, the further definitions of such a material existent thing which are found in a Thomistic ontology present no problems. As we have said, *materia* is for St. Thomas the *principium individuationis,* the principle of quantity, of the *motus,* and so in the end of actual time (in contrast to *historicality* as this must be conceived in the *aevum* of the angels or in a certain sense in the utterly supra-temporal setting of the freedom of God). Thus both the method and the results of this piece of metaphysical anthropology may be taken as Thomistic.

The second observation to be added at this point refers to

---

[3] See In VIII *Met.* 1, 2, n. 1287.

[4] Assuming with St. Thomas that the angels are pure immaterial existent things. The factual and biblical correctness of this assumption is not under discussion here.

[5] For an extensive treatment, see *Spirit in the World,* pp. 91ff., 311-366.

the question already examined. Why is it precisely the assumption of the materiality of the knower that is a metaphysical explanation of the possibility of a receptive knowledge of an object that is distinct from the knower? It may not yet have been made perfectly clear what the assumption of a purely non-specific real possibility in the knower might itself contribute to this purpose. It could be objected that our deduction of the materiality of a receptive cognition by means of the dialectical manipulation of the concept of a receptive cognition and of the proposition about the being present to itself of the existent thing has established nothing more than a verbal equation of the two pre-conditions. In the pre-conditions the "thing other than the knower" which is supposed to be the initially known object of a receptive cognition is really distinct from the knower himself. But this is known by the receptive cognition. By contrast, however, the result of our deduction is that the "thing other than the knower," beside which the cognitive existent thing exists ontologically, is the empty possibility of the *materia,* that is, an *interior* factor of the knower's own reality. One might think that we had wrongly denoted two totally different things by one and the same phrase, "the thing other than the knower," in which the knower is understood as existing and as knowing in like manner. It is true that the other thing known is a determination of the object that is distinct from the knower, whereas the "thing other than the knower," in relation to which the knower exists ontologically and in which he is supposed to subsist, is the *materia prima.* Nonetheless, our deduction is valid, as may be shown in various ways. Let us choose the simplest if not the most fundamental proof. Let us proceed from the scholastic axioms, *"Motus est actus moventis"* and *"Motus est in moto."* The effect of one existent thing upon another which subsequently results in the substantial constitution of both the active thing and of the thing that it determines, is the reality of the active thing itself (that is, its own specification); it is this reality in such a way that it can be so specified only in the thing that it determines. Let us apply this to the ontological determination of one who knows through his senses. This determination is the reality of the sensible object itself, *motus est actus moven-*

tis; it has its reality within the medium of the one who knows through his senses, and is thus at the same time a reality proper to the one who knows through his senses. It is both *his* determination, and the determination of the thing known who shows itself through his action. If this object is now known in the knower because it is the knower's determination, then at the same time a reality is grasped that is the determination of the sensible object itself. But if such a determination could be the reality of a moved and of a mover (in our case of a knower and of a thing known that determines the knowledge), then the precondition for this is the materiality of the mover and of the moved. For Thomistic ontology this is immediately obvious. *Motus* in the true sense is conceivable only in what is material. This concept is open to examination, and the proof of this necessity follows the same lines as our earlier proof of the necessity of the materiality of a receptive knower. The region of the possibility of the contact between the mover and the moved is the non-specific, empty, and yet real possibility which utterly permeates all material essences and appears in space, not as multiple and repeated, but as the self-same, empty, quantitative unity, which is as such neither one that can be multiplied nor yet a unity which excludes an unlimited distribution of its component factors. The *materia* is one and many within the dimension of substantial principles, as space within that which comes into sensible appearance. There are not many "spaces," for all are but parts of the one space, and yet there is not just one space which is able to maintain its unity against unlimited discreteness. It is the same with the *materia* which is indeed the principle of the interior spatiality of an existent thing. It is not *many* within the many existent things as though it were repeated as the same thing over and over again in the particular existent things, nor yet is it *one* in such a way that it excludes a separating out into the many of the many existent things. Hence it is able to be the medium, the otherness as such, in which a mover and a moved communicate in *one* determination as that of unity. All spatiality in which the action, as determination of the active agent, takes place is likewise the spatiality of the thing determined, because it is the manifestation of the *one materia* in the sense stated. The otherness, in

137

which two existent things participate in common through their subsistence in the one *materia,* is the condition of the possibility of a determination of the "existentness" of the one being and that of the other also. Without this common medium of an empty "being other" which in itself is one, it would not be possible for a specific uniqueness with respect to *"quidditas"* to be at once that which is proper to the active agent and that of the other that is determined. When an ontological reality gives way of its own accord, by becoming the reality of another non-determined particular expression of the *materia,* straightway a determination of another existent thing, which maintains itself in this very *materia,* becomes its own actuality. Should the one be grasped, then the determination of the other is receptively known.[6] In short: because the *motus* can be both the *actus* of a *movens* and of a *motum* only where there is *materia,* so too it is only in the material order that a receptive knowledge is possible. This is knowledge in which a determination is that of the

[6] It has been presented earlier that in this givenness of that which recognizes through the sense to the other of the *materia,* the strange other can be recognized *as* an other. Besides, the *materia* is strictly speaking not simply the concrete other upon the meeting of which man, in his giving away of himself, opens himself to the *materia,* but the domain within which such a meeting is possible. In the pure giving away of himself to an *empty* otherness man would still remain within himself, not really immediately divorced from himself. Man in his materiality, therefore, enters into the domain of his existence-completion, a domain already determined by the *concrete other;* for it is only in that he always already enters into the concretely determined other of *materia* and experiences its determination (*forma*) as his *own* reality, that he is truly "with the other" in his own existingness (without this being again, simply the pure negativity of his being-with-himself). This concrete otherness, precisely because it is always executed as one's *own* determination from the basis (*forma*) of one's own being (*motus* as *actus moti*), can only be experienced as the one not in our hands, as the "truly other," when it (this otherness) is understood as coming from a *free* other basis (*forma non mere materialis, sed subsistens*). This in turn again implies, from another point of view, the transcendental deduction of a plurality of the co-world of free persons as regards man. Also derived from this is the fact that the transcendental foundation of a *surrounding* world of man can only happen as the moment of a foundation of the transcendental necessity of the personal *co*-world, no matter how obviously other persons seem to be merely things among others as seen in the light of ordinary *a posteriori* perception. See J. B. Metz, "Mitsein," in *LThK* VII, pp. 492f.

determining object which acts and yet can be known through itself. It is the determination of the knower as the existent thing that is acted upon by that which is known.

Having made these supplementary observations we now return to our theme proper. This analysis of man in history so far has been undertaken with the intention of producing a philosophy of religion. We wanted to find the place of a possible revelation of the free God for men. We have recognized man as that existent thing who in virtue of his absolute transcendence stands in free love before the free God of a possible revelation. At the very start of our enquiry about the place of a possible revelation we said that the absolute transcendence with respect to being in general must be a basic characteristic of this place of a possible revelation. Were this not so, the place of such a revelation would be a restricting *a priori* condition governing the content of revelation, and this would be contrary to the genuine concept of revelation. We also said that such a revelation might have to be expected in words. Finally, it was ascertained that if the place of a possible revelation is to be specified as Word more precisely than merely in terms of the absolute transcendence of the human spirit, this can come about only in the sense that the *human* character of this transcendence (and hence the character of a word of God that is audible to man) can be made clearer. The purpose of our undertaking was to present the nature of man more explicitly. We in fact discovered his historicity. But we are still not at the end of our road. We must still ask what this historicity has to do with transcendence. What we were actually trying to do was not to find the characteristics in the nature of man, but the characteristics of his absolute transcendence. So far, it has still not become clear why and to what extent the historicity of man determines his openness to the God of a free and possible revelation, nor how this turns this openness into a *human potentia oboedientialis* towards such a revelation.

12. SPIRIT AND HISTORICALITY:
Being and Appearance

In order to make plain the essential connection between the transcendence of the human spirit and the historicity of man, we must first of all recall how this historicity was discovered. It was not discovered as a mere *datum* but as the result of a transcendental deduction from a character of the human spirit itself. Historicity was derived from characteristically human spirituality and it is thus the historicity of the human spirit as such. We now have to examine the significance of all this.

Man possesses his transcendence (that is, his vision of being in general) in virtue of his being receptive cognition. Receptive cognition, however, has proved itself to be interiorly sensate. And so man knows about being in general only through sense perception. We must not understand this statement in the sense that man, possessing this knowledge through the senses, as spirit subsequently comes to see what he is capable of with this sense knowledge and the objects grasped through it. It is precisely in its sensate, material character that knowledge through the senses has proved itself to be the necessary condition of this transcendence with respect to being in general. This in its turn possesses its openness only through the self-disclosure to sense perception of a single object. That is to say that man's sense perception is correctly conceived only as corresponding to the spirit and its necessity. That spirit which in itself and despite its transcendence is a *tabula rasa* must, in order to achieve the fulfillment of its own nature, produce out of itself a sense perception as its own faculty. A spirit of this kind enters into the *materia* in order to become spirit. Man enters into the world in order to stand before being in general which is not com-

140

pletely expressed in the "existent-ness" of the world. Such a conception of human sense perception is completely in harmony with Thomistic epistemology,[1] which conceives sense perception explicitly as a faculty which arises out of the spirit in its self-examination of its own intrinsic nature—to be openness to being in general. But precisely because man's sense perception must be conceived not as something existing of itself, but essentially as a faculty of the *spirit,* it follows that the spirit possesses its openness to being in general (and hence to the absolute being of God) only in and through the possibility of an encounter with materially existent things in time and space through its penetration of the *materia.* And so for man as finite and receptive spirit there is a luminosity of being in general only in the encounter with the material. There is an approach to being in general only in the approach to materially existent things. There is access to God only in a penetration of the world. And insofar as the access to God is given only in the *a priori* structure of the human spirit (that is, only in its own proper transcendence or a return into itself), we may assert that man possesses the possibility of a return into himself that reveals being, and hence God, to him only in an out-going into the world of which man himself is a part.

If we speak in this context of materially existent things, the concept must not be restricted to present things that provide the immediate object of our outward senses in virtue of their sensible qualities. We must allow the concept to include all that can be presented directly to a receptive cognition. Thus we have in mind not the outward sensible objects alone but also man himself, insofar as he grasps himself through the cognitive and active dealings he has with the concrete, existent reality of which he is a part. We may use a single word to denote all of this— "world." Insofar as these "things" that make up the world are objects of a receptive knowledge they must necessarily reveal themselves and appear automatically in their own nature. We may, therefore, describe all of this as "appearance," but without wishing to declare thereby that what is grasped receptively in

---

[1] See *Spirit in the World,* pp. 243ff.

this way is mere illusion. By "appearance" we wish to express first of all that these objects *appear* in themselves and are not simply known in virtue of a cognition of something else; second, that in these immediate objects of a receptive knowledge, being in general becomes a *datum* through the pre-concept and thus *appears* in them and only in them. In receptive knowledge the world appears as it is to the extent that finite human spirit can grasp it. "Being," which is always more than the "existent-ness" of the world, is thus revealed in the world.

Thus we may formulate our present question in these terms. What is the precise relationship between the appearance and the openness of "being in general" in the transcendence of the spirit?

To begin with, we must remind ourselves of what we have said already concerning transcendence. Man occupies his place in the surrounding world not simply as a movable piece of that world, but as a self-subsistent person distinct from an objective world of which he is a part. By making judgments and initiating activity, he differentiates these "objects"[2] intrinsically from himself. In this way, the human mind possesses the possibility of a return into itself, a return into a conscious subsisting in itself. In this self-subsistence it grasps the "objects" through concepts, through a universal review of what each proposition expresses. Every proposition always predicates a universal *"quidditas"* or "thisness" of a subject. We have already shown how the pre-concept with respect to being in general is the transcendental condition of the possibility for this self-subsistence and universal, conceptual, and objective grasping of existent things encountered in the world.

[2] If the personal co-world is here called "objective," this should not lead to prejudice concerning the closer characteristics, cognition and personal self-givenness. In mentioning love (above p. 123) as being an inner moment of the contingent (and yet absolutely to be affirmed) reality, we have already given a certain view to the analysis of this particular kind of personal cognition. Yet the basic question remains, whether the attempt here entered upon might not have to be repeated anew with an *initial* and *continuing* viewing of the original and underivable peculiarity of personal being-with and the way of appearance and cognition given herein. This question is of course at the same time related to the attempt of thomistic metaphysics of cognition.

It has now become evident that we must not think of this pre-concept as some kind of innate idea of being in general, still less as an objective intuition of an idea of being that exists in itself, or even as the absolute being of God himself. Any of these ways of thinking of it would contradict the proposition that man's knowledge is receptive in origin. If we were to think of the pre-concept in any of the ways mentioned, then man would be in possession of a material knowledge that would be utterly independent of sensible, receptive cognition of a particular object in the world, that is to say, utterly independent of appearance. The pre-concept as such is hence no *a priori* knowledge of an object, but the *a priori* horizon of perception of an object presented *a posteriori*. It is the *a priori* condition of the knowledge of an *a posteriori* appearance. It is not a self-subsistent grasp of being in general, but the pre-concept of being that is possible only in the comprehension of the appearance.

We are now in a position to define more precisely the relation between transcendence and appearance. We can distinguish three factors in an objectively grasped appearance.

(1) The appearance, insofar as it is given us through a sensate and receptive cognition. That is, the sensible object in the world insofar as it forms our material sense-receptivity by its own activity and thus makes its appearance.

(2) The vision into being in general opened up through the pre-concept. Because sense perception has shown itself to be a faculty of the spirit the particular sensible object is grasped from the very start by man's cognition in the dynamic striving of spirit towards being in general. As a result, in the grasping of the sensible object the pre-concept itself comes into action. It becomes conscious and thus, through its own unlimitedness, opens up to the spirit the unlimited breadth of being as such. In the grasping of the appearance, being itself is grasped by anticipation in its ever expanding breadth.

(3) The appearance, insofar as it is grasped at all, is grasped through the pre-concept with respect to being in general. It is not as though the appearance in its sheer sensile givenness was alone present to human consciousness and that concurrently a glimpse opened up into being in general. In a transcendental deduction

143

we showed how the pre-concept is the condition of the possibility of grasping appearance in a specifically *human* manner, that is, under universal concepts and in the self-subsistence of the knower. That means, however, that the sensible object is, as it were, informed by the pre-concept and by the knowledge of being in general which it opens up. A synthesis arises between the purely sensible appearance and the knowledge about being in general that is opened up in the pre-concept. The appearance is grasped as an existent thing *sub ratione entis*. And it is only through the appearance's being grasped as an existent thing that man is granted knowledge of being in general.

And so we have three factors: the sensible appearance as such; the knowledge of being; the existent thing as the synthesis of sensible appearance and knowledge of being in general.

The first two factors appear at first in direct knowledge only in their synthesis in the existent thing. Were this not so, then sense perception and the pre-concept would have to represent two faculties in man, each having to grasp an object on its own and independently of the other. This is impossible as far as the pre-concept is concerned, because of the receptive character of human knowledge. It is ruled out, too, for sense perception, on account of its being a faculty which arises out of the spirit as something proper to itself.

Applying this in reverse, we see that it is now even clearer that there are three aspects of our general problem of being. Being is grasped as the "act of existence" of an existent thing. It is at once separate and united to a receptive subject that is distinct from it. This is but another way of expressing the fact that in the pre-concept we grasp being only through the concept of a specific, sensibly presented, and particular existent thing. Being and existent thing are not the same, for being is the ultimate goal of the spirit in its absolute transcendence. It is the condition of the possibility of knowledge of an existent thing and involves a differentiation between "act of existence" and "subject" which cannot rest in being alone. For man's finite receptive knowledge, being is grasped only in the reception of a sensible object which is seen as a part of the movement of the spirit to being itself. Being thus appears as "having being" in the measure of the essence of the known object.

To the extent, therefore, that the pre-concept and that which it reveals become known only as appearance in the sense that this forms a horizon, which by its presence indicates that there is a "beyond," we have proved the utterly unlimited breadth thus implied to be the condition of its being able to turn the purely sensible appearance of an object as such, into an *object* of man's transcendental knowledge.

This essential reaching out of spiritual cognition beyond the sphere of appearance by turning towards it, corresponds to the same ontological subsistence both of reality *(forma)* and of *materia.* In the same way, the pre-concept likewise permanently reaches out beyond the world to being in general, and yet has being only in a grasping of the appearance of the world.

We may say, therefore:

(1) Being in general is disclosed to man only in appearance. This first became perfectly clear with respect to knowledge applied directly to the objects of sense perception. The objectivity of being as distinct from the self-subsistence of the human subject is conditioned by the pre-concept. Man knows about being in general even in such cognitions and such active dealings with his world. He knows about it insofar as such knowledge is the preparatory condition or horizon of objective conceptual knowledge of material things. These are the initial starting points and hence also the permanent basis of all his cognitions. Thus it is that man, even in his transcendental reflection upon these conditions of his direct objective knowledge, remains ever dependent upon this starting point. It may well be that in the course of such reflection the object of knowledge is changed, but never its structure and hence never the way in which these objects have to be grasped. Even if being, insofar as it is *not* restricted to the world as a possible totality of appearance, is objectively conceived, it must be conceived through and in the manner of an object in the world, in the manner of an appearance. Being in general, and all that is immaterial, we conceive in the manner of material things. We conceive it as a subject (the *materia*) of

145

which an intrinsically universal *"quidditas"* is predicated, that is to say, as an existent thing which "has" being. We are in no position to conceive a thing existing in itself, in any other way. Here we see, as a result of our attempt to think of being in general and in its absoluteness, the uncommutable origin of all of our concepts in receptive knowledge through the senses. Expressed in Thomistic terms our first proposition would run: *Nihil sine phantasmate intelligit anima*. Even if we are obliged to comprehend something which according to its own essence cannot appear in time and space (because it is not a material thing), and so cannot show its true self through receptive cognition, still it cannot be comprehended by man apart from reference to an appearance through which this non-material thing becomes a *datum*. We have still to define this more exactly. And so being, both in direct knowledge and in metaphysical reflection, can be grasped only through an appearance.[3] Even tran-

---

[3] With the word "apparition" we of course mean all the various kinds of phenomena that are experienceable in the world-realm; for the world of apparition must be conceived as to begin with as the co-world of man. Therefore the sentence in the text above may not be misunderstood, as if metaphysics were exclusively and foremost possible when turning to those models of contemplation which are got from physical experience of things. Ontology happens much rather *primarily* in the turning-to those phenomena which become visible in the thing that "is" ontology, in *man himself*. And because we are concerned here with a turning-towards the "phenomenon itself," this turning-towards may not simply be equated with the abstracting view of the abstract entity that is "man"; rather, what is meant is the turning-towards man as a "concrete phenomenon," which contains the whole of his history, and history itself as moving still towards a future not yet reached. See J. B. Metz, *Christliche Anthropozentrik* pp. 16, 43ff., 97ff. Here it also becomes clear the magnitude of the diastasis between being and phenomenon is different in each case, and that this diastasis itself also has a history, corresponding to the historicity of the phenomenon ("man"); this in turn implies a history of the "ontological difference" itself as the formalization of the difference between being and phenomenon. We might touch briefly upon the question whether and it what sense the formal horizon for "ontological Christology" could be discovered in this connection, inasmuch as God's promise of himself to the world has its apex in Jesus Christ in whose humanity—as being and history—it reaches *ultimate* eschatological appearance. See "Zur Theologie der Menschwerdung," in *Schriften zur Theologie* IV, pp. 137-155.

146

scendental reflection upon being as a whole is effected necessarily through objects.

(2) It is in appearance that man finds *being in general* opened up to him. Not every existent thing that can be said to "have being" can appear in itself to a receptive cognition. For such a cognition is essentially sensate and hence demands a sensible, material object through which to be determined. But a material object is spatial. Hence whatever is not spatial cannot in itself appear to a receptive cognition. And yet being in general can be disclosed to man in appearance. In our analytic of man as spirit we have already shown that in the pre-concept that goes beyond the appearance, being in general is disclosed to the spirit as an objective grasping of appearance. In the pre-concept at least the most general structures of being in general, that is, all that is attributable to being, are simultaneously known. These most general structures which are attributable to being as such are called the transcendental definitions of being. We have already given at least some hint of these. Being is being-present-to-itself. Being is knowing or luminosity. Being is self-affirmation, the will, and the good. In the first place, therefore, at least in a general way, being in general is disclosed to man by appearance insofar as these most general definitions of being in general are known. Obviously, much more might be said about them than we have here expounded. But now the question arises: can a *particular* existent thing, which in itself has no appearance, be known by a cognition which has the structures of receptive cognition? In other words, can the non-appearing existent thing be made to appear by intra-mundane appearance taken in its most general, non-specific structures only? Or must it appear in its specific, absolutely particularized character?

Certainly, we have already recognized a specific non-appearing existent thing in a concept which is attributable to this alone—God. We defined his essence as that of the existent thing of absolute "having being." Of necessity this concept can be proper to one only, to this one we call God. But if we recall how the necessity of affirming a divine existent thing arose, it is easy to see that we have known God only within a general

147

doctrine of being and epistemology as the condition of the possibility of any finite existent thing and its affirmation. In this way, we have merely a knowledge of God as a function of the world and its special existence. To speak with St. Thomas, God is thus not the *"subiectum"* of a special science which is able to enquire about him directly, but he appears only as the *principium subiecti* of the science of the general doctrine of being.[4] But our enquiry is in fact directed towards discovering whether a non-material and non-appearing existent thing (in particular God) is able to show itself by means of appearance, in such a way that its being and action have not already necessarily been shown by this same appearance.

Only when we have answered this question are we at the end of our search. The question asks, in fact, where the place is in man of a possible revelation of God. So far we have answered by saying merely that it is his transcendence which is his historicity, or objectively, the appearance of the world to him through being. But this is not everything. We have to ask now whether appearance is able to grant only a vague glimpse into the general structure of being in general and thus of the non-appearing existent thing, or whether this existent thing might possibly be capable of becoming known even by appearance in its particularity. We must not take this question as though it presupposed that man's knowledge is able on its own to go beyond the general structure of being in general and grasp a supernatural [5] existent thing in its concrete particularity. The pre-concept unveils "the beyond" from appearance only to the extent that this is necessary for the objective grasping of the appearance itself. For the conscious self-subsistence of man in the world, such a thing is *a priori* impossible. The disclosure of the most general structures of being is perfectly sufficient for the pre-concept in this sense. Our question is not concerned with the

---

[4] For an extensive treatment, see *Spirit in the World*, pp. 387ff.

[5] Until now, this being has been characterized purposely as *non*-appearing. This primarily negative formulation served repeatedly to call attention to the fact that this "super-worldly" existent is given for the recognition of man immediately and from himself only as a negative liminal experience.

possibility of man's knowing by his own power what is beyond this world in its concrete characteristics through appearance. But we must ask whether at least *from the side of God,* through the means of appearances, an other-worldly existent thing might be unveiled in its concreteness; whether appearance, apart from its unveiling of being in general, is capable of being used to unveil further the character of being, or whether such an unveiling of its character is possible only by way of circumventing and excluding appearance and hence the normal mode of human knowledge.[6] Only if we are able to accept the first alternative does it become clear that man may look for a revelation from God upon ground upon which he already finds himself standing. This is the ground of transcendence as historicity.[7]

[6] We would like to point out once again that here—as in the general context—the following question is not entered upon: in what way such a categorial-verbal revelation, regardless of its power of relating the truly non-phenomenal in its peculiar self-determination, is nevertheless, and rather in this way only, nothing but the categorial-reflexive, historical coming-to-itself of that enlightenment by grace of the subjectivity of man, which takes place in the self-revelation of God to this subjectivity. Of course we must not lose sight of the fact that such a categorial reflexion, in its genuine historicity as the inner-worldly-verbal occurrence of revelation comprehends *itself,* and that these events of the reflexive thematization of the revelation belong to the event of the one ever-whole divine revelation—that here "thematization of revelation" betokens both subjective *and* objective genitive.

[7] And this answer at the same time takes up the third moment of the basic relation of transcendence and phenomenon (see above, p. 177).

13. THE HUMAN HISTORICITY
of a Possible Revelation

We shall answer the question just posed in a proposition that
at the same time is the third of the propositions in which we
tried to formulate the relationship between the transcendence of
man and his existence in the world. (3) All existent things can
be made objective *through the word* within the horizon of mundane appearance. This proposition—the most important of all
for further discussion about the philosophy of religion—requires
more thorough exposition.

To begin with, we must focus our attention on two well-
known facts. In the pre-concept the horizon for being itself is
opened up. Thus we already know of positive determinations [1]
of all existent things. On the other hand, every existent thing
is not able in itself to become a *datum* of a receptive cognition.
How, then, can such a thing become known in its specific
character? The answer at first is, through *negation*. To understand this properly we must first of all recall the analogy of
"having being." An existent thing may not be conceived as the
sum of properties as though each of which was self-contained,

[1] The transcendental-liminal experience of the "other-worldly" does
not mean that this "other-world" thus experienced is given only in
empty absence without content (something that every *simply* transcendental presence would abrogate again). The positivity which consequently comes into being in every transcendental-liminal experience,
cannot, however, be separated from its transcendental negativity, in a
way that what has been separated could simply bypass this negativity
and be understood by and in itself in this sense. Yet it is precisely the
original positivity of being that shows itself in transcendental liminal
experience (see p. 81) in the way that it does not simply arise in the
existingness of the individual (materially grasped) existent and con-
sumes itself in it.

and was joined together with the others in a purely external way. That which we call the characteristic of an existent thing is nothing but an expression for the mode of "having being" of an existent thing. This "having being" can be defined by negation, and so knowledge of a particular existent thing can be arrived at, even though it is beyond the world of appearance. For on the one hand, through the pre-concept we grasp, even if in an empty fashion, *a priori* all possible modes of "having being" from the mere possibility of the *materia prima* to the absolute "having being" of God. On the other hand, specific modes of "having being" become immediately and palpably accessible to us in appearances. Through the negation of the limit of any such particular and immediately accessible "having being" and through the removal of the upper limit in the direction of the absolute being of God, supra-mundane existent things can be defined, at least negatively. This definition is in some sense specific and not merely in those most general determinations, which they have in common with all existent things. This definition arises in and out of their relationship to the immediately known modes of "having being." (By "supra-mundane existent things" we understand not just substantial essences as such, but also facts about them, etcetera.) Because the concept of the "existent thing" is no mere static concept of empty generality and non-predication, but on the contrary possesses an inner dynamic towards the perfection of "having being" in God (this is the real meaning of what we said about the analogy of "having being" and hence about the concept of the existent thing), it therefore carries within itself the possibility of growing and becoming fuller from within and not through the addition of external properties derived from elsewhere. But this provides us with the possibility of allowing the concept of the existent thing along with its transcendental determination to emerge and grow until it denotes a specific supra-mundane "having being." The limit to this process is set by the original definition by negation. Insofar as positive content of such a concept is always gained from and remains dependent on appearance, the seeking after appearance in this attempted extension of knowledge of a supra-mundane existent thing by means of negation never becomes inane. We can illustrate this with an example from geometry. Imagine a given area as the region of reality, and then imagine a defined sector of this area, in which fixed points are accessible at will independently of each other. Then starting from these points, we can determine and define unambiguously any chosen point in the whole area through its relationship to these immediately accessible and fixed points.[2]

[2] These considerations are directed to the comprehension of the possibility of a fact that in itself is already known in advance (and because the transcendental deduction of a possibility can and may have as a prerequisite the historical experience of its factuality, this procedure cannot be illegitimate). Thus in the paragraph above the factually ensuing, verbal relation that has always been categorially mediated is known in advance—and precisely in the way in which it presents itself in the immediate, "naïve" perception of faith: as a sum of individual statements, guaranteed by God's authority, about matters which are unapproachable to man within the limits of his experience in the world-horizon. If one sets up this immediate material perception of revelation of the word as a precondition and asks immediately upon doing so, how these individual statements *singly* are able correctly to state a fact above and beyond experience, then such considerations on the positive stateability of truths beyond experience will be attempted by means of the analogy of the concepts used and unfolded in the text above. Of course one could also proceed methodically in such a way that one begins by thematizing more precisely the sense of the individual statements and their meaning by theological principles. In this case the result would probably be that *factual* Christian revelation does not actually represent any matters of fact about the other world in its "in itself" *un*related to us, but always the relationship of God to the world as absolute nearness of divine self-revelation or the concrete action of God upon this our world, inasmuch as it has its own quality of phenomenon in it. (In this fundamental relationship to the world of the content of revelation, to say the least, there is contained already an apparently so radical reality, divorced from earthly things, as the trinity. See "Ueber den Begriff des Geheimnisses in der katholischen Theologie," in *Schriften zur Theologie* IV, pp. 51-99, esp. 82ff. The angels, too, need not be thought of as simply "other-worldly" in this context, in that their existence could be known only through such a revelation centered immediately upon them. See "Angelologie," in *LThK* I, pp. 533-538. Finally, one must not forget that the so-called "absolute" attributes of God are in every case understood on the basis of the transcendental qualities of the understanding of being, and in this sense do not stand in a simple non-relation to the world.) But under these preconditions the gnoseological problem approached in the text could be put in yet other terms: revelation would not *at first* appear to be a categorially strewn revelation of word, but as the event of the one self-revelation by grace of God in man and his open spirituality; one could therefore start with the

This is not at all the same thing as saying that every existent thing in the supra-mundane sphere of ontological possibilities can be comprehended in its inner possibility by man on his own and through the objects that are directly accessible to him. The reason for this is simple. The actual existence, at least, of the supra-mundane existent thing depends too upon the free delimitation of God, so that man on his own is unable to predict this existence. The same thing may hold good, in special cases at least, of the knowledge of the sheer possibility of such an existent thing outside the world of appearance. For if, when several negations come together within the concept of such an existent thing, this existent thing is to be presented at all to human knowledge, then it is conceivable that out of this same concept the possibility of such an existent thing can no longer be known. At the same time, however, the concept actually still governs this existent thing definitively, thus allowing knowledge of it. In the geometrical illustration we used above, the field of being in general in its unlimitedness was experienced only as the lack of a *specific* limit in the pre-concept, not in its infinity in itself. For man this field is not specifically known and so it may be that the definition of a real or imagined point in this field outside the intra-mundane sphere in terms of two or more points in the sphere of experience does in fact aim at a point which no longer happened to fall within the field. In other words, we might not be sure whether it denoted an impossibility or not. But if this doubt is removed by a revelation or in some

---

concept of a gracious "transcendental revelation," and it could probably be shown that the categorial factual revelation of Christianity is nothing but the reflexive thematization of this "transcendental revelation" and that it therefore has its legitimization actually already in the factuality of this "transcendental revelation" and its categorial, necessary self-representation. Inasmuch as man, of course, always finds his place in the concrete historical exegetical condition of his transcendentality (enhanced through grace), takes this exegetic condition as basically legitimate and precisely because of this may not make his own "private" interpretation of this transcendental experience to the decisive criterion of human transcendental experience; in this regard the point of departure taken in the text above is also necessary and inavoidable, if the danger of subjecting the salvation-historical "official" revelation is finally subjected to a purely human criterion of revelation is not to be inadvertently incurred.

other way, a true cognition of such an existent thing may be possible by means of this sort of negative definition.

So far we have ascertained the following: all existent things are fundamentally definable in terms of the sphere of appearance. This definition can be achieved only through negation. This definition does not mean that man can achieve it on his own in such a way that all existent things can be known by man in their inner possibility or even in their actual existence. On the other hand, it has already been established that a supramundane existent thing cannot be, in itself, a receptive cognition. All of this says no more than that a supra-mundane existent thing can be presented to a finite spirit through the word. In this connection we do not give "word" the meaning which we gave it earlier, to denote a mere representative symbol of some kind or other. We now mean the *conceptual* symbol of the spirit directly applied to this thing. The only possible place for a negation is in the word, which obviously is not the same thing as a mere phonetic sound.[3] Accordingly, the whole of supra-

[3] This negation is first simply given by the word "not" and thus really shows by itself that it can be materially given only in "the word." But this "not" is, first of all, the thematization of that negating distinction which is given with every determinate and thus always delimiting statement, if it is not be simply "not-saying" anything; but it can also be the thematization of the "not" of transcendental liminal experience on the whole, and can *therefore* be used also for the thematization of supernatural reality: if for example certain determinate characteristics are subtracted from God ("God is not worldly") without such a negating sentence being simply the abrogation of a statement about him that says nothing; for such a sentence always implies too the positive quality of content of the transcendental liminal experience and attempts to make just this positivity present in its "not." Besides, this "not"—though less explicitly, still necessarily implicit—is also given in statements which make an indialectically positive assertion about God in pure grammatical terms ("God is just"); this is possible because by means of a particular word ("God") the instruction is always given to man to co-accomplish the negating transcendental liminal experience in the hearing of such a word or, more exactly: to understand the predicate ("just") of a sentence, in which such a word ("God") is subject, as the categorial locus from which the transcendental liminal experience is to be accomplished. This categorial locus of the transcendental liminal experience (in our example: "just," "justice") is not at all irrelevant for it itself. For if this categorial locus were of no account, if it could be

mundane existence is capable of comprehension in the word. For, on the one hand, the word does not represent the existent thing in itself, and on the other, through the negation which it is able to bear, it has the possibility of defining even those existent things that are outside appearance, in terms of appearance. The human word, insofar as it always bears a reference to an appearance, hence can be the mode of revelation of each existent thing. Insofar as the human word as bearer of a concept gained through negation of a supra-mundane existent thing is heard as spoken by God, it is able to reveal the existence and inner possibility of such an existent thing.

Summing up our three propositions we can say: through the human word, which is the bearer of a concept of a supra-mundane existent thing gained from appearance through negation, this existent thing can be opened up to man.

We have already seen that man is the one who must of necessity listen for a possible revelation of the free God. To the extent that it has now become evident that even supra-mundane existence can be revealed through the human word, we are now able to say also that man is at least the one who must listen for a revelation from this free God speaking in *human words*. To the extent that it has become obvious that the human word does not imply any *a priori* restriction of the content of a possible revelation, no limitation of God's freedom is involved if we say that what he likes lies within this waiting for such a word. We need enquire no further at this point whether God is able to reveal himself to man without the assistance of a word, such that something supra-mundane is presented through the negation of appearance. In any case, this would be possible only through the annulling of the already established structure of human knowledge which is a unity of spiritual transcendence and sensible appearance. Because man of necessity knows himself only as this kind of creature, he has no cause to wait for a revelation that might possibly arise through the annulment of this unity.

---

transferred at will for the one liminal experience, this experience itself would not be able to bring any kind if positivity into being at all, it would be the "not" purely by itself. See above, chapter 9, note 3.

Thus we need not bother to discuss the possibility of such a revelation. Still less have we occasion to do this when it has become evident that any such revelation would in the end have to be transformed into the kind of inner possibility which we have just described. For as long as man still remains within the limits of the ontological structure which we have described he must always translate any other kind of revelation into this structure, if that revelation is to determine his normal being and acting. In other words, revelation must be contained in human speech.

In the first instance we had only to answer the question as to the relation between transcendence and historicity. That which we called "appearance" now turns out to be nothing other than those things which man encounters in the course of history. It denotes the whole of intra-mundane existence, not just the objects directly open to sense perception, but also man himself in all his being and action, this same man who comes to know his own historical essence in his knowledge of an inter-action with his world and environment. We have now answered this question at least to the extent that we are able to say: all supra-mundane things can be presented to man, not just in their most general ontological definition, but also in their specific attributes, by negation through that historical appearance which we call "word." This "word" is in turn itself the synthesis of an intra-mundane, historical objectivity and a transcendental negation. The word is thus ascertained to be the *locus* of a possible revelationary encounter with the free God before whom man constantly stands by virtue of his transcendence.

This has not made sufficiently plain, however, the relationship of man as an historical creature to a possible revelation. True, it has been ascertained that man must pay heed to a word which may possibly proceed from God, this word that will be spoken in human speech and that yet is able to say all that might possibly be revealable. But still it is not clear *where* man is to wait for this word. This leads us on to another question.

In order to answer this question we must unite two of the pieces of knowledge we have already acquired: the insight into the historicity of man and the historicity which intrinsically attaches to a possible revelation from God.[4]

Let us start with the historicity which attached *intrinsically* to the revelation of God. God's revelation is grasped as the free act of God towards men, for which there is still a possibility, and with which man must always reckon. This presupposes on the one hand the finitude of man, on the other his absolute transcendence or delimitation of man by God. Such a free act of God which takes place within the truly receptive place that is a human being, is already historical in itself. It is not prehistorical, like the creative delimitation of human being, which was free and with God when he was acting only with himself.[5] This is not universal and necessary either, because being free, it is not predictable, but always capable of discovery and comprehension only in terms of itself. For it there is no point or precondition within which it can be defined in its actuality and individuality other than God's free act. And so it remains always an unexpected thing, in spite of all the calculating and waiting. Thus in itself such free revelation is historical. It is the unique self-subsistent action of a free person.

How, then, does such an action of God occur within the

[4] We only touch upon the fact here that the question would have to be put more decisively, to what extent revelation as history from the point of view of God and revelation as a historical occurrence from the point of view of the historicity of man once again are internally related; that is, to what extent "divine history" and "the historicity of man" are already formally and previously to factual supernatural history of salvation, materially related to each other. Does there exist "history with God" belonging to the essence of man (as a creature endowed with spirit)? If so, in what sense then is the "*a priori* history" with God the most inner determination of the historicity of man himself, so that both would not simply have to be harmonized with one another after the fact, but could be seen from the start in such a way that the one ("historicity of man") can be understood in its essence only when it is understood from the other ("history from God"), and vice versa? Of course both the God-world relationship as well as the problem of the historicity of man himself would have to be taken up under aspects that cannot be pursued in detail in the course of this work. It will be useful, however, to refer to chapter 1, note 15, chapter 2, note 3, as well as note 5 below.

[5] See above, chapter 6, note 3, and chapter 9, note 5.

sphere that is man's? In spite of its divine historicity can it be humanly *un*historical? Can it fail to occupy some specific point in space and time within human history, or must it, on account of its divine historicity, also occupy a specific place in human history, impinge upon the human historical process at a precise point in time and space, so that man is obliged to turn towards this specific point if he is to hear the word of God's revelation? We maintain that it is the second alternative that corresponds to the inner nature of a possible revelation from God. We have already mentioned *one* reason for this.[6] The revelation of God, whatever its origin, must in the end be translated into human speech, if man is not to be completely taken out of his human mode of existence by it. Thus if we may not assume that God's revelation is going to snatch man up out of his natural mode of thought and action in a miraculous way, then at least within individual human existence free revelation can appear only at a point. For the rest of his life man can preserve the revelation only in its form in human speech and in so doing must refer back to this special point in his individual history as the humanly

[6] Of course the answer to the question as it is posed in what follows, could be given in greater detail and compass, and this especially given the possibility (or even actuality) of that which has been called "transcendental revelation" in earlier notes and which is co-extensive to the total history of mankind. It does not at first appear at all self-evident in the light of this possibility that the factual divine revelation has a spatial-temporal placement *within* this total history of humanity and does not simply coincide with the event of this total history as such. But it could be shown that this "transcendental revelation," precisely in order to reveal its true freedom, its inderivable originality and in this to be understood *as* revelation in the sense of the inderivable free affirmation of God, sets itself necessarily in history in such a manner as to set itself off intra-historically from other events of this one factual history of humanity. Of course, inasmuch as, inversely, this "transcendental revelation" ever enlightened by grace is not simply something differentiated from the transcendence of the human spirit and its formal historicity, but *itself constitutes* this differentiation and encompasses and preserves that which has been set off within it as different, the total history of mankind in which the human spirit consummates and objectivates itself nevertheless remains also a history of revelation determined by grace. See "Theologische Anthropologie, in *LThK* I, pp. 618-627; "Weltgeschichte und Heilsgeschichte," in *Schriften zur Theologie* V, pp. 115-135, and J. B. Metz, "Weltverständnis im Glauben," in *Geist und Leben* 35 (1962) pp. 165-184.

unique point in which God's revelation was originally given. In the human-historical way too, therefore, revelation occurs at first in the sense that it is not able to be co-existent in equal permanence with all the separate elements in an individual human history. So in order to grasp revelation man has to refer back at least to certain special points in his own history through an historical memory. Having come so far, there is no difficulty in principle arising from man's having to reckon with the possibility that such a revelation might not occur in every individual history of each man, but only in the history of *special* individuals. It makes no essential difference in these circumstances whether he has to refer to a point in his *own* history or to a point in that of some *other* man—it is only necessary that he is able to recognize that a true revelation has been given at this point in human history. A real difference would arise only if the man had to be able to repeat at will in his own life this revelation in its original expression. Then indeed the outward historical ascertainment of an original experience of revelation by another man would be no substitute for an interior experience of revelation in one's own life. This assumption is in fact contradicted by the *free* divine historicity of revelation, at least on the presupposition that man is to be left with the mode of being that we have already established even when he becomes the recipient of revelation. The historicity of possible revelation in itself must thus be conceived historically in the sense of a *human* history, that is, it is expected to be an event fixed in time and space, within the total history of mankind.

Thus the only question that arises is whether each man is able to hear it should it appear at some point in human history that is very remote from him. In this study we do not take this question to mean: how does the individual man actually and concretely acquire knowledge of such an historically given revelation? Our question is, rather, a transcendental one. Why does man *a priori* in virtue of his nature need to indulge in a factual investigation of history to find out if a revelation has been given? Why may he not simply maintain from the start an attitude of indifference to human history in general, so that the attempt at a factual proof of a given revelation could find no

a priori possibility of reception in such a man? Further, this
question is not posed in that sense of asking whether a man has
to reckon in general with a revelation by God in virtue of his
own nature, for we have already answered that. The question
is simply as to why man because of his nature must reckon with
a revelation by God in human history. The proof from the
nature of the case that revelation must be given in history if it
is given at all, is not a sufficient answer to this question, for it
is a question not about revelation but about a peculiarity to
which revelation is supposed to be addressed.

Our question approaches the subject *from the human side*:
why, as one who listens for a revelation, must man necessarily
listen within *history*? We have already laid the foundation for
the answer to this question too. Man is an historical creature.
He is this in and on account of his transcendent openness to
being in general, his openness to God and so to a possible revelation. In order to stand before being, man must turn to appearances. As we have already stressed, appearance is not simply
particular sensible objects of external sense perception but the
whole of mundane existence, including a man's own history and,
insofar as a man is always one of humanity, the history of humanity also. Turning towards history is thus not an attitude for
man to adopt as he pleases, but is imposed upon man by his
specifically human spirituality. Any conscious breaking away
from his history would be an inner contradiction of his specific
nature, not just to the extent that this has its biological side,
but precisely because of its spiritual side. In that turning towards
appearance which is of the essence of every human cognition,
man constantly corroborates the turning towards something that
is basically historical. This is because appearance, at least as
actuality in man's life, is unique and factual. Hence all rationalism, as the attempt to give human existence a non-historical
foundation, is to be rejected as non-human and therefore un-
spiritual as regards the human spirit. If on the one hand man
has to be spirit, but cannot be spirit unless he turn to appearance, then he may not remain disinterested in the greatest possible and richest appearance, in the greatest possible sum total

160

of appearances. For the wider and more varied these are, all the more do they manifest that which is the goal of the spirit —being in general. Man himself, however, is the appearance with the greatest fulfillment in itself. He is that appearance which is able of itself to provide the appearance that most matches up to being itself. But what man is itself appears only in the unfolded reality of possible human being within the history of man in general, in the history of humanity. Thus, to be spirit, man is essentially, in virtue of his spiritual nature, orientated towards history. If man stands before the God who freely reveals himself; if this revelation has to occur in human history if it occurs at all—for indeed if it failed to occur the most essential thing in human history would be the discernible silence of God; if man is from the start orientated towards this history in which this revelation may possibly occur, then in his essence man truly is that existent thing who, at the core of his essence, is attentive to a possible revelation of God in human history. Only he who thus listens, and only to the extent that he thus listens, is that which he specifically has to be—man. And so metaphysical anthropology becomes the ontology of the *potentia oboedientialis* for a possible revelation. Hence the philosophy of religion is the analytic of man's attentiveness to a possible gratuitous revelation. All natural religion, however, that might be construed with the assistance of such anthropology and metaphysics, would have grasped its own nature only if it were itself that self-comprehending listening for and reckoning with a possible revelation of God in human history.

This concludes the third round in the study which we undertook at the introduction to the third aspect of the problem of being. In concluding we are able now to formulate the *third* proposition [7] of our metaphysical-religious-philosophical anthropology. Man is that existent thing who must listen for an historical revelation of God, given in his history and possibly in human speech.

[7] See the formulation of the first and third propositions on pp. 67 and 108 respectively.

Having achieved this we believe that we have answered the essential basic features of the question which we posed at the beginning of our study; and now at last we are able to sum up this solution in anthropological terms, so that we may say with a certain definitiveness: man is the existent thing, possessing a spirituality that is receptive and open to history, who stands in freedom and as freedom before the God of a possible revelation which, if it occurs, appears in his history (as the supreme actualization of that history) *in the word.* Man is the one who listens in his history for the word of the free God. Only thus is he what he must be. Metaphysical anthropology has thus reached its conclusion when it has comprehended itself as the metaphysics of a *potentia oboedientialis* for the revelation of the supernatural God.

Having said all this we have scarcely even touched on many of the questions that might arise in connection with such an ontology of the *potentia oboedientialis* for a possible revelation. Let us merely draw attention to some of these, by way of an appendix. There is still to be answered, for example, the question as to how a human word spoken in history can be recognized as the speech of the supernatural God. In terms of our previous problems we would have to say: because the human word is intended to apply to a supra-mundane existent thing by an appearance, through negation, becoming a pointer to this supra-mundane existent thing, this negation must demonstrate itself to be objectively valid, and not merely resting upon an arbitrary definition by man. Proceeding from this as starting point we would then have to work out a metaphysical concept of *miracle,* which *a priori* would cover not merely its purely physical side as the suspension of a law of nature, but in terms of a basic account would reach down to its character as a *sign* [8] of the God who reveals himself. Breaking the confines of the mundane context is *a priori* to be regarded as a sign addressed to man who is already listening for the revelation, and which through the negation of this *closed* natural context attests the objectivity and

[8] See "Zur Theologie des Symbols," in *Schriften zur Theologie* IV, pp. 275-311.

162

positivity of the negation which occurs in the word of revelation.[9]

Another question would be bound to arise concerning the concrete manner in which the historical experience of the individual man can penetrate to the historical event of a revelation, especially if this revelation, measured by the external measure of time, is far removed from this individual man. We would have to analyze more exactly the historical determination of the individual spiritual life. In so doing we would most probably come up against the problem of the temporality of the spiritual history of man, of a temporality which is not simply the application of stellar time to the physical course of human history, but a more basic and unique category that precedes, and is independent of, physical time. Thus the historical link between a particular man and a "past" event (according to physical time) might perhaps display itself as a human-historical "simultaneity." It would appear that events in human history as such do not occur in the same sense and in the same rhythm of physical sequence as physical happenings. We would have to examine the metaphysical concept of *tradition* which is of basic importance to the spiritual-historical nature of man. For man's turning back to a "past" history takes place in the fundamental sense not through historical studies but by this past remaining present in a living tradition (measured in human-historical time), indeed by its still existing. If these and other concepts of human historicity were to be elaborated they could then be applied to the history of revelation, note being taken, of course, of the modifications which they undergo through entry into divine-human history. At the moment, we must content ourselves with these general indications.

[9] See "Heilsmacht und Heilungskraft des Glaubens," in *Schriften zur Theologie* V, pp. 518-526; see also J. B. Metz, "Wunder, Wunderglaube," in *Lexikon für Pädagogik* IV, Freiburg, 1955, pp. 1018-1020, and "Wunder," in *Der grosse Herder*.

PART FIVE
CONCLUSION

14. THE PHILOSOPHY OF RELIGION
and Theology

It now remains for us to set the result of our research explicitly within that context in which we viewed our question in the first two chapters.

First of all, in the first chapter, we occupied ourselves with an examination of the relationships between the philosophy of religion and theology. In that study we proceeded from a scientific and theoretical viewpoint. Our intention was to define two sciences in terms of their relationship to one another. This cannot be achieved by looking for this relationship as they are now, but only in terms of their primary constitution and origin.

From the very start it has been evident that theology, in the Catholic sense of the hearing of the personal revelation to man by the free God who is superior to the world, cannot be worked out by man, but must always rest upon the fact of such a *Logos* of God himself. All the sciences except theology are in a real sense anthropology. That is to say, they are all, in spite of their application to things, based upon man's *Logos* in respect for their "that?" and "how?" They are "things in the mind of man." Theology exists solely because there is a word from God to man. It is true that in theology, too (in its total procedure), we can distinguish two elements: the simple hearing of God's message,[1] and the systematic elaboration of what is heard in formal categories which forms part of human historical spir-

---

[1] Naturally, the whole of human spirituality in its concrete historicity is at work in the simple hearing of the word of revelation; an *adequate* differentiation between positive and systematic theology is therefore not feasible. See "Theologie im Neuen Testament," in *Schriften zur Theologie* V, pp. 33-53.

ituality itself. This second approach is in itself *primarily* a human operation. In this the message from God that has been heard, to some extent becomes a "thing" on which man reflects using the formal principles by which he seeks to grasp intellectually anything that is presented to him. Certainly, any such theory of the science of theology would still have many questions to answer: the possibility and purpose of such an intellectual-systematic elaboration of God's message, the limits of such activity, its methods, its relationship to theology in the first sense, and so on.

When we speak *here* of theology, however, we mean theology in the first sense—the *kerygma* itself, the simple hearing of the word of God itself, the believing acceptance of the message itself. We do not mean the metaphysical reflexion upon what is heard and believed, insofar as and to the extent that a metaphysics which has become thematic (even in the kerygma itself) can make such theological reflection possible and distinguish it from positive theology.[2] It is true to say of such positive theology that it exists not because man thinks but because God has spoken. Distinct from every other science, in positive theology it is God who appears, and not the nature of man. Nonetheless, even in such a science man cannot be completely overlooked and excluded, because there would be no word of God were there no one who was at least intrinsically capable of hearing it.[3] Thus there is a theological anthropology, not just in the specific or strict sense that God himself in his *Logos* reveals to man the ultimate structure of his own human essence, so that a theological anthropology is a part of the *content* of theology; but in the sense that an unreflective, perhaps naïve, self-understanding by man is the condition of the possibility of theology at all.[4]

The hearing of a revelation presupposes a definite basic constitution of man and must consciously affirm this revelation as free hearing. The word of God, in order to be audible from its

[2] See J. B. Metz, *Christliche Anthropozentrik,* pp. 101ff.
[3] See chapter 1, note 8.
[4] As regards the "formal" meaning of anthropology for theology, and the related question regarding an "anthropological direction of theology" on the whole, see "Theologische Anthropologie," in *LThK* I, pp. 618-627.

past, must itself go forth as human speech, and once again this presupposes this definite constitution of man. And so it appears that theology has to presuppose for itself a *theological* anthropology which we might call "fundamental-theological anthropology," and which can appear materially as of the substance of *theo*logical anthropology. The studies we have been pursuing so far are nothing more than this very fundamental-theological anthropology which, insofar as it was pursued as metaphysical science, contains the root of the totality of metaphysics.[5] And now in conclusion two questions emerge. (1) What is the relationship between this fundamental-theological anthropology and the traditional concept of the philosophy of religion? (2) If the two sciences mentioned are identical at least in their core, what is the relationship of this philosophy of religion, defined as "fundamental-theological anthropology," to theology?

(1) The answer to the first question is along the following lines. Genuine philosophy of religion is a fundamental-theological anthropology of the kind we have tried to pursue in its external outlines. What we are engaged in is anthropology insofar as we are concerned with man. Insofar as we see man as that creature who has to attend in freedom, within his history, to a possible message from the free God, it is *theological* anthropology. It is fundamental-theological anthropology insofar as this self-understanding which man has of himself is the presupposition for the fact that he is able to hear at all the theology that has actually arisen. This fundamental-theological anthropology is the

---

[5] Since metaphysics—on account of the historicity of its thought—must, notwithstanding its peculiar method, be pursued with a view historical pre- and self-cognition that has ever been consummated in the existence of man, a materially adequate delineation between theology and metaphysics is neither an ideal, nor can it be effected concretely. Metaphysics, then, can most certainly consider theological data without giving itself up. Of course this does not mean to say that a fundamental-theological anthropology which understands itself to be a "theological" discipline in the strict sense, would not materially be more than that metaphysical anthropology of *potentia oboedientialis* for a possible revelation as it has here been developed in its outlines. Yet this metaphysical anthropology is rightfully so "theological" itself, that it is materially identical with a fundamental-theological anthropology to a great degree. See J. B. Metz, *Theologische und metaphysische Ordnung.*

169

philosophy of religion proper. This fact must be demonstrated in a little more detail.

First of all, we proceed from the common idea of the philosophy of religion which, in the formal neutrality of its definition, apparently still has nothing to say about this apparently startling thesis that for us as believers and philosophers, the philosophy of religion in its true, full, and substantially definite concept is and can be nothing other than this very discipline which we have named "fundamental-theological anthropology."

The philosophy of religion in the literal sense is first of all the philosophical definition of what religion is and has to be. Thus the philosophy of religion is philosophy, that is, it works with the means of cognition which are proper to philosophy in general. It defines religion in terms of a position that is antecedently and always fundamentally accessible to it. It defines it by reason of the unalterable essence of man, of the world that is of necessity presented along with man, and by reason of the clear and necessary formal basic laws of thought, all of which we are accustomed to describe as "the natural light of reason." [6] In such a way we will now try to define the essence of religion. We have neither the opportunity nor the intention of enumerating the various results that have been achieved from such attempts in the course of the history of thought. It is sufficient for us here simply to ascertain that a philosophy of religion which aims at being more than a mere description of the cultural phenomenon of religion, and wishes to enquire into the truth about the essence of the complete would-be religion, must arrive at least at a knowledge of the absolute and personal God who is above this world. It thus recognizes religion as the existential bond of the whole man to this God. All empirically ascertainable religions are religion only to the extent that they truly achieve this existential bond between man and the living God.

From this formal definition of the philosophy of religion and

---

[6] This characterization of philosophy must not be understood as adequate; otherwise the historicity of philosophy too, its relationship to the factual order of grace and revelation as well as their function within theology, and so forth, would have to be described more closely.

170

of religion, the first thing that emerges is that the philosophy of religion contains within itself a metaphysical anthropology. That it does so obviously does not imply that metaphysical anthropology and the philosophy of religion are formally indistinguishable, and thus are one and the same thing. But it does mean that in its propositions at times one science essentially and necessarily posits the other. This is so for two reasons. First, the philosophical knowledge of God (the kernel of a normative philosophy of religion) is possible only within the bounds of the one metaphysics. The *theologia naturalis* is not a philosophical science based upon itself, having only the principles of formal logic in common with the other philosophical disciplines, but is an inner factor of the general doctrine of being, of metaphysics. But general ontology is always metaphysical anthropology. In general ontology the topic under review is being in general, not in the sense of the empty, logical uniformity of the "something" (a concept that could never cover a definition of the absolute being of God that would be adequate for a philosophy of religion), but in the sense of an ontological concept of being which can indeed be affirmed of all existent things. This affirmation is made in such a way, however, that it always includes the awareness of what "having being" really is in its growing purity and fullness, and so that this concept is known to be predicable only analogically. This is possible only if the philosopher at some stage directly reaches at least one existent thing which in some way is itself open for this perfected "having being," that is, spirit. In order to practice ontology, man must have comprehended himself as spirit. Only then is he able to know what "having being" really is analogically. That amounts to saying that a general ontology and thus a *theologia naturalis* are always already inherent in anthropology—in a man's knowledge of himself. The philosophy of religion is *theologia naturalis,* but this is possible only in a more original and permanent unity with metaphysical anthropology.

The connection between the philosophy of religion and metaphysical anthropology appears more simply and plainly from the fact that the philosophy of religion, as the systematic inter-

171

pretation of the existential bond between man and God, must know not merely about God, but also about man who is supposed to be bound to God. All philosophy of religion is hence necessarily an affirmation also concerning the nature of man and is implicitly metaphysical anthropology.

So even on the basis of a formal and apparently neutral definition the philosophy of religion shows itself to be metaphysical anthropology.

Such anthropology which is an inner factor of the philosophy of religion of necessity becomes fundamental-theological anthropology in the sense defined earlier. For this metaphysical anthropology which we have studied with purely philosophical tools, showed man to be that existent thing who necessarily stands in freedom before the God of a possible revelation. It showed that such metaphysical anthropology is fundamental and theological. Whatever else such an anthropology may decide about man, certainly it cannot ignore this essential characteristic. And if the philosophy of religion deduces from anthropology what man's religion ought to be in the eyes of God, of necessity it will also have to indicate that man must be ready to hear the living word of the free God within his own history.

In short, whatever else it might be in itself the philosophy of religion will always be a fundamental-theological anthropology, the final word of which is the systematization of the necessity which directs us to listen for the word of God. And because such a word has in fact been spoken, philosophy of religion is not required to do more than to sketch out this sort of fundamental-theological anthropology. For whatever it might make of man's religion by the rational light of reason, the philosophy of religion would always be surpassed by revelation. Speculations by the philosophy of religion do not have the same existential importance that they would have if God had not himself spoken and man had been left listening to the silence of God. Such knowledge of an intrinsically possible philosophy of religion is not philosophy and metaphysics in the same sense as is provided by fundamental-theological anthropology—that is, if by philosophy and metaphysics we understand not simply thought

172

about anything and everything, but an activity of man's existential predicament.[7]

(2) Thus we are now in a position to define explicitly the relationship between the philosophy of religion and theology. The philosophy of religion exists where it is what it should be, namely, fundamental-theological anthropology. This fact expresses its true relation to theology. It is only philosophy; but it is *human* philosophy. Hence its original, interior, first and last act is the open readiness for theology. It is never able to coerce theology or to calculate what it will be. It can impose no laws upon theology. But it constitutes an existent thing which is able to hear should the *Logos* of God enter this world. Because he has come and must always be heard, its task ever remains that of the *"facienti quod in se est Deus non denegat gratiam"* within the sphere of knowledge. This is intrinsically a moral judgment, in the same sense as we are accustomed to use this phrase so that the above theological axiom is correctly applied to it. The philosophy of religion is therefore not the same thing as theology, but is practiced upon a different level or using other means of knowledge, or it is something which constructs a purely hypothetical order which would apply were there no theology at all. It is the constitution of the human readiness for theology, and as such its necessary presupposition. It is the constitution of the *potentia oboedientialis* for revelation, carried out in the strictness of scientific research.[8]

Why, then, we go on to ask, does the philosophy of religion as fundamental-theological anthropology leave theology to be *exclusively founded upon the word of God itself?* No further

---

[7] Such speculations either drift into the actual material theology of revelation in order to gain there a genuine existential meaning, or they incur the danger—because of their will to "pure philosophy"—of having philosophy of religion take itself to be the self-enclosed constitution of the true religion, and thus sink to the level of mythology.

[8] In this we do not deny but rather include the fact, that grace—revelation—theology, in an essentially historical process, sets as a precondition of itself the unity of nature—transcendence—philosophy, and therein sets itself free. See J. B. Metz, *Theologische und metaphysische Ordnung.*

lengthy discussion is needed to answer this problem. The philosophy of religion as the knowledge of man as unlimited spirit facing the God of a possible revelation cannot pre-judge the possible content of such an utterance of God. It cannot even pre-judge the question whether such an utterance has occurred. The religion of actually existent revelation through the word of God leaves the question of the listener to the speech *or* silence of God entirely within itself. Because man's listening must reckon equally upon God's silence, God's self-revelation remains in every respect incalculable and unmerited grace. It is true that listening to God is the condition of hearing the word of God, and this listening is the free act of man in his true existential self-understanding. There is, first of all, no actual hearing that is necessarily linked with the listening. Perceiving the silence of God can also be an answer, made meaningful by listening, because man can become what he must be even through God's silence. He is a personal, finite, and historical spirit standing before the personal, infinite, free God, with whom he can have an "historical" contact at least by negation. And further there remains the mystery of the actual self-constitution of the listener as the concrete act of man who is autonomous and free, even when subject to the free grace of God. Thus the actually accomplished constitution of the condition of the hearing of theology was itself a free act of God before it was man's. Because God himself thus produces the readiness to listen as condition of hearing his own word, theology is purely and simply founded upon itself. It is the word of the living God himself. The philosophy of religion precedes it only as condition that is itself created by God's speaking. It is a condition of theology which is heard by man and which itself is conditioned by the word of God.

In this way we have defined the relationship between the philosophy of religion and theology insofar as this can be made evident from the standpoint of the former. As we explained at the very beginning, we have not attempted to examine the problem from the other side. Let us briefly illustrate these results by a reference to those questions by means of which we clarified the problem in Chapter 2. There were three questions: the usual method of fundamental theology, the question as to the possibility of a Christian philosophy, and the basic types of Protestant philosophy of religion.

(1) In the usual method of fundamental theology we failed to see any explicit discussion of the question as to how man could be the place for revealed knowledge without this already being due to him as the necessary *telos* of his immanent development. We saw no discussion as to how man might be seen as the possible hearer of an unexpected word of God, and at the same time be necessarily compelled to listen for this unexpected word within his history. These questions of fundamental theology have now, it is hoped, been answered at least in outline. Thus our fundamental-theological anthropology was in fact that piece of fundamental theology that was customarily omitted, or at least not explicitly stated, namely, the analysis of the *potentia oboedientialis* for revelation.

(2) It has become clear also to what extent philosophy as such is and can be Christian in the original sense. It is not primarily because theology is its protecting *norma negativa* or compels it to take up the metaphysical elaboration of theological problems. This activity would better be described as scholastic theology than as philosophy. Philosophy, as genuine philosophy, is Christian when, as fundamental-theological anthropology, it loses itself in theology. Indeed, insofar as it is the constitution of man as a listener for a possible revelation from God, it always becomes merged with theology. For even presupposing that God keeps silent, the man of such a metaphysics does hear a word of God in this silence. Even in this case the final existentially decisive attitude of man should be a bowing before this silent God, and in a certain sense man would be the theologian of an historical utterance of God concerning human life. Even the silence of God would be an "expression" and hence in this sense a "message" about the unique, undeducible, free relationship of God to man. That is to say, it would show God turning away and keeping to himself. And so human philosophy is always constituted by its readiness to surrender its existential, basic character in favor of a theology, thus losing itself in the sense already explained. Philosophy, rightly understood, is al-

ways a *praeparatio evangelii* and is intrinsically Christian—not in the sense of a retrospective baptism, but because it forms a man who is able to hear God's message to the extent that he can do this for himself.

(3) Finally, we can now understand also why and how a Christian philosophy of religion in this sense is the genuine and original unity and synthesis of the two basic types of Protestant philosophy of religion already mentioned.[9] Our philosophy of religion as fundamental-theological anthropology on the one hand shows a positive receptivity of man for revelation. It is no mere negative, dialectical counter-attack to the simple criticism of all that is human and mundane. On the other hand, it possesses this receptivity not merely as something that in view of revelation becomes another way of expressing a demand for fulfillment of this religious receptivity which has God as its necessary and immanent objective. On the one hand, God is really able to speak, and on the other hand man is able to hear the unpredictable word of God, in such a way that it is really perceived. Our discussion has surely proved that intellectualism, rightly understood (that is, intellectualism that sees man as free, historical spirit, who must perfect his spiritualization within a "world" and with reference to the absolute spirit), is less in danger of humanizing revelation as a process belonging to man's nature, than is any philosophy of religion which makes feeling or some such thing the special seat of religion. If man is an historical spirit facing the free God, then on the one hand he is open to a positive fulfillment of his *potentia oboedientialis,* which as spirit he necessarily possesses. Revelation thus need not be a mere criticism of all that is human and simply "other-worldly," never capable of becoming flesh but always remaining a thorn in the flesh. On the other hand, he can and must accept the free revelation of God as unexpected, unmerited grace, that is, as *history,* this is not contrary to nature, but is certainly as supernatural.

We have reached the end of our examination of the problem. It may seem as though we have accomplished but little. But

[9] See above, pp. 25ff.

let us for a moment presume that we have genuinely succeeded in accomplishing the little that we set out to accomplish. Having done this we have traced out upon the theoretical plane what a man must do in the realm of existential decision when he sets out in search of an answer to the question as to whether or not the living God desires to meet him in his own life-history and the history of the human race. If we have achieved that much, then we have had decisive success. Let us assume that a man is convinced that it is part of the most essential basic attitude in life to seek the decisive word of God's personal self-revelation somewhere in the concrete here-and-now of human history. This word is decisive and compelling to man in the strictest sense of his personal existence. Let us assume further that man is convinced that such a word of God which ought to be the existential foundation of his life must come essentially within human history. It will be veiled, that is, resembling human speech in form and exposed to all the contingency of scandal of an historical event. But before the forum of reason with its eternal ideas it is clear from any angle. Such a man, we might suspect, convinced of these above propositions, has already traversed the most essential part of the road to the Christian faith of the Catholic Church, insofar as the intellectual element of a living decision is involved. Any such man must expect from the start that he can and must reckon with an historical religion that is attainable only through the reception of and turning towards an historical space-time situation. This situation will not be resolvable into rational propositions, that is, it will not be simply the outcome of a religious sentiment or experience or of anything else that forms the basic structure of religion. In the end, precisely because it enters human historicity as the revelation of God, it will possess all the contingency and all that is intrinsically ambivalent and be open to all the doubt and confusion that is inevitably found in a human historical phenomenon. Anyone who takes unbiased account of these things will find it difficult not to recognize the holy Roman Catholic Church as the seat of the genuine revelation of the living God.

When we consider the application of this claim by the Church to all non-Christian religions, we first observe that all modern historical attempts to level down Christianity to but one among many phases and forms of man's religious structure, proceed not from an *a posteriori* ascertainment of the actual identity between Christianity and other religions, but from the more or less explicit *a priori* assumption that there can be no revelation of the living God in some particular chosen place in human history. It is also assumed, *a priori,* that there can be discussion only about the means and not about the fact of the need for a history of all religions in which all be brought to a common denominator since a *supernatural* history of one religion in distinction to others is *a priori* ruled out of the question. The genuine parallels that can be established *a posteriori* between Christianity and non-Christian religions are all explicable, without the assumption of this false, *a priori* principle of modern history of religion, by means of one simple fact. This is that man is the same the world over, and that where man's expectation of a true revelation from God is not satisfied or not thought to be satisfied very easily, comparable substitute images begin to arise.[10] Anyone, however, who does not share this *a priori* prejudgment, and has not lost heart in advance in the search for the absolute within the finite, will not find it hard to ascertain the essential qualitative difference between Christianity and every other form of religion. It will not be difficult to recognize the Church as the *signum elevatum in nationibus* which has

[10] After all, in order to judge the religious-historical parallels, one must keep in mind that humanity—because of God's universal will for salvation—factually stands under the affirmation of supernatural grace as a whole, and is therefore (at least initially) incorporated into the horizon of the one history of revelation, since grace (as the supernatural self-revelation of God) and revelation are not related by chance and by mere exterior disposition, but are related in essence (see above, chapter 2, note 6). But from this it is clear that, even in the non-Christian sphere, the liminal experience—which is truly preserved actually only in the light of grace—of the "expectation" of an historically arriving divine revelation can articulate itself as a knowledge disposed by God, so that this liminal experience can objectivize itself as a genuine and totally encompassable religion, and, thus involved, can represent that historical event of revelation which has found its own unique, unsurpassable, and lasting presence in the *signum elevatum* of the church. See "Das Christentum und die nichtchristlichen Religionen," in *Schriften zur Theologie* V, pp. 136-158.

already proved itself to be the seat of God's revelation. Here we presuppose that such a man adopts an attitude which reckons upon a possible historical revelation of God. This attitude certainly is the presupposition of a man's being able to see Christianity as qualitatively different. Otherwise, a man with *a priori* pre-judgment will make demands of the historical phenomenon of Christianity which obviously it can never fulfill, for it is the history of God being expressed in *human* history.

What now of the relationship between the Church and other forms of Christianity? These other Christian Churches are not an answer to the human limiting experience of an expectation of revelation because they no longer have the courage (which they must once have had) to regard themselves in their own historical uniqueness as the exclusive place of God's revelation. We can speak of an historical revelation of God only if this historical manifestation is the cause of a claim to *"extra ecclesiam nulla salus."* This is a claim that it is the sole historical, visible entity which to the exclusion of all others is the place where a free God can adequately be found. It is where religion, as an actually achieved bond between the whole man and God (which man could never have worked out for himself), is really present. When man ceases to dare to make this claim, when man at the very most shows only a slight preference for the Christian form of religion, he has given up the historical unambiguity of the word of God and with it the courage to believe in a genuine, historical revelation of God. In short, whoever reckons with the possibility that a specific portion of human history, to the exclusion of others, may be God's history,[11] is bound to believe in revelation in the Catholic sense. The demonstration of the necessity of reckoning with such a possibility we saw to be the kernel of the Christian philosophy of religion and the key to its most essential relation with theology.

[11] And here, of course, this "piece" of divine history may *not* be thought of as simply *any* phase *next to* other phases of history *within* an encompassing historical process, but as its historically founding reason itself. See "Weltgeschichte und Heilsgeschichte," in *Schriften zur Theologie* V, 115-135; see also J. B. Metz, "Die 'Stunde' Christi," in *Wort und Wahrheit* 12 (1957), pp. 5-18.

Having thus arrived at the end of our discussion, we discover the end to be a fresh starting place. At this point we could and ought to set about a fundamental recapitulation of our whole thesis, a recapitulation which approaches the purpose and form of a Christian philosophy of religion from the angle of theology and its understanding of itself.